UNITED NATIONS OFFICE ON DRUGS AND CRIME
Vienna

Global Report on Trafficking in Persons 2012

UNITED NATIONS
New York, 2012

Comments on the report are welcome and can be sent to:

Global Report on Trafficking in Persons Unit
Research and Trend Analysis Branch
Division for Policy Analysis and Public Affairs
United Nations Office on Drugs and Crime
PO Box 500
1400 Vienna
Austria
Tel: (+43) 1 26060 0
Fax: (+43) 1 26060 5827

E-mail: globaltipreport@unodc.org
Web: www.unodc.org

PREFACE

Human trafficking is a crime that ruthlessly exploits women, children and men for numerous purposes including forced labour and sex. This global crime generates billions of dollars in profits for the traffickers. The International Labour Organization estimates that 20.9 million people are victims of forced labour globally. This estimate also includes victims of human trafficking for labour and sexual exploitation. While it is not known how many of these victims were trafficked, the estimate implies that currently, there are millions of trafficking in persons victims in the world. Human trafficking requires a forceful response founded on the assistance and protection for victims, rigorous enforcement by the criminal justice system, a sound migration policy and firm regulation of the labour markets.

However, if the international community is to achieve long-term successes in combating trafficking in persons, we need reliable information on the offenders, the victims, and the trafficking flows throughout the regions.

The *Global Report on Trafficking in Persons 2012* provides such information, and explores this crime across the world. Although the officially reported information that forms the basis of this report cannot be used to generate a global estimate of the number of victims, it has shed light on the patterns and flows of human trafficking, in line with the request of Member States. The Report provides a solid basis for understanding the global nature of this form of modern slavery. Its findings are deeply troubling.

According to the Report, at least 136 different nationalities were trafficked and detected in 118 different countries. Human trafficking happens throughout the world with millions of victims falling through the cracks of their own societies only to be exploited by traffickers. They can be found in the world's restaurants, fisheries, brothels, farms and homes, among many other activities.

One of the most worrying trends is the increase in child victims. From 2003—2006, 20 per cent of all detected victims were children. Between 2007 and 2010, the percentage of child victims had risen to 27 per cent. Trafficking originating from East Asia also remains the most conspicuous globally. Based on the Report, East Asian victims were found in 64 countries in all regions, and were often detected in large numbers.

Another worrying aspect is the low conviction rates. According to the Report, the conviction rates for trafficking are at the same level as rare crimes such as homicides in Iceland or kidnappings in Norway. We, therefore, need to work harder at detecting and punishing this shameful criminal activity.

Aside from these negative developments, there were some positive trends. By 2012, 134 countries and territories had enacted legislation criminalizing trafficking. Indeed, the percentage of countries without an offence criminalizing this activity halved between 2008 and 2012. There is also evidence that trafficking from Eastern Europe and Central Asia has been declining since 2000.

Overall, the international community has the tools to confront this crime. The widespread ratification of the *Protocol to Prevent, Suppress and Punish Trafficking in Persons, Especially Women and Children* is a success story. Currently, 154 countries have ratified it. The Protocol is closely supported by the *Global Action Plan of Action to Combat Trafficking in Persons*, which also established the *Trust Fund for Victims of Trafficking in Persons, Especially Women and Children* to aid the victims.

Although much has been achieved, gaps in knowledge remain. UNODC continues to need additional information about human trafficking. The Report is a stepping stone in the right direction, and it highlights the dedication and commitment of Member States to tackle this crime, but I call on countries to do more. We need comprehensive data about offenders and victims in order to assist in the development of sound policies and appropriate criminal justice responses. Human trafficking is a widespread crime in the early 21st century, it cannot be allowed to continue into the 22nd century.

Yury Fedotov
Executive Director
United Nations Office on Drugs and Crime

Editorial and production team

The Global Report on Trafficking in Persons 2012 was produced under the supervision of Sandeep Chawla, UNODC Deputy Executive Director and Director, Division for Policy Analysis and Public Affairs.

Global Report on Trafficking in Persons Unit
Kristiina Kangaspunta (Chief), Fabrizio Sarrica, Raggie Johansen.

Human Trafficking and Migrant Smuggling Section (chapter 3)
Ilias Chatzis (Chief), Alexia Taveau.

Studies and Threat Analysis Section (layout and production)
Suzanne Kunnen, Kristina Kuttnig.

Cartography
UNODC and Atelier de Cartographie de Sciences Po.

The Global Report on Trafficking in Persons Unit would like to thank Thibault Le Pichon (Chief) and Anja Korenblik of the Studies and Threat Analysis Section for their valuable guidance and support, as well as Julia Kuzmits and Gaetano Lo Mastro for assistance with the data collection and data entry.

The report also benefited from the work and expertise of many other UNODC staff members in Vienna and around the world.

CONTENTS

Text boxes

FIGURES

MAPS

TABLES

KEY FINDINGS

- Women account for 55-60 per cent of all trafficking victims detected globally; women and girls together account for about 75 per cent.

- Twenty-seven per cent of all victims detected globally are children. Of every three child victims, two are girls and one is a boy.

- In general, traffickers tend to be adult males and nationals of the country in which they operate, but more women and foreign nationals are involved in trafficking in persons than in most other crimes.

- Women traffickers are often involved in the trafficking of girls and tend to be used for low-ranking activities that have a higher risk of detection.

- Trafficking for sexual exploitation is more common in Europe, Central Asia and the Americas. Trafficking for forced labour is more frequently detected in Africa and the Middle East, as well as in South and East Asia and the Pacific.

- Trafficking for the purpose of sexual exploitation accounts for 58 per cent of all trafficking cases detected globally, while trafficking for forced labour accounts for 36 per cent. The share of detected cases of trafficking for forced labour has doubled over the past four years.

- Victims trafficked for begging account for about 1.5 per cent of the victims detected globally. Trafficking for the removal of organs has been detected in 16 countries in all regions of the world.

- Victims of 136 different nationalities were detected in 118 countries worldwide between 2007 and 2010.

- Approximately 460 different trafficking flows were identified between 2007 and 2010.

- Between 2007 and 2010, almost half of victims detected worldwide were trafficked across borders within their region of origin. Some 24 per cent were trafficked interregionally (i.e. to a different region).

- Domestic trafficking accounts for 27 per cent of all detected cases of trafficking in persons worldwide.

- The Middle East is the region reporting the greatest proportion of victims trafficked from other regions (70 per cent). Victims from the largest number of origin countries were detected in Western and Central Europe.

- The trafficking flow originating in East Asia remains the most prominent transnational flow globally. East Asian victims were detected in large numbers in many countries worldwide.

- Victims from Eastern Europe, Central Asia and South America were detected in a wide range of countries within and outside their region of origin, although in comparatively lower numbers outside their region of origin.

- Almost all human trafficking flows originating in Africa are either intraregional (with Africa and the Middle East as their destination) or directed towards Western Europe.

- One hundred and thirty-four countries and territories worldwide have criminalized trafficking by means of a specific offence in line with the Trafficking in Persons Protocol.

- The number of convictions for trafficking in persons is in general very low. Notably, of the 132 countries covered, 16 per cent did not record a single conviction between 2007 and 2010.

EXECUTIVE SUMMARY

The present *Global Report on Trafficking in Persons 2012* is one of the outcomes of the United Nations Global Plan of Action to Combat Trafficking in Persons, adopted by the General Assembly in 2010. The General Assembly tasked the United Nations Office on Drugs and Crime (UNODC) with data collection and biennial reporting on patterns and flows of trafficking in persons at the global, regional and national levels, to be carried out in close collaboration with national authorities. The present report is the first of its kind and marks the launch by UNODC of a series of global reports on trafficking in persons.

Previous UNODC reports on trafficking in persons have highlighted the lack of knowledge with regard to this crime and called for Member States and the international community to increase efforts towards obtaining a solid understanding of this complex crime of global reach. Some progress has been made. While the overall picture remains incomplete, as the capacity to detect and report on trafficking in persons continues to vary greatly from country to country, the pool of information available for researchers to draw upon has increased significantly in recent years. As a result, the findings presented in this report rest on an objective and relatively solid evidence base, although significant information gaps remain.

Following the mandate of the General Assembly in the Global Plan of Action to Combat Trafficking in Persons of July 2010, the purpose of this report is to inform about human trafficking patterns and flows. For that, UNODC has based the analysis on a large sample of officially detected cases of trafficking in persons world wide. While this serves the purpose of assessing patterns and flows of trafficking, it cannot be used as a base for estimating the level of crime or number of victims (see textbox in Chapter II).

On the basis of mainly open source information, the International Labour Organization (ILO) estimated that 20.9 million people are victims of forced labour globally. This estimate includes victims of trafficking in persons; however, the number of victims of forced labour as a result of trafficking in persons remains unknown.

The report consists of three main chapters. Chapter I presents a global overview of the patterns and flows of trafficking in persons, including the profiles of the offenders and victims, the forms of exploitation that traffickers employ and the nature of the myriad flows of trafficking victims that criss-cross the globe. Chapter II presents more detailed overviews of regional trafficking patterns and flows. Where the data allow, the regional sections are broken down into subregions to facilitate an even more detailed analysis, as the crime of trafficking in persons often has distinct features in specific geographic areas. Chapter III discusses the efforts countries have made to combat trafficking in persons and the progress that has been made since the Trafficking in Persons Protocol[1] entered into force in 2003.

Further material is available on the website of the Global Report on Trafficking in Persons (www.unodc.org/glotip). The website includes country profiles of all 132 countries covered as well as a methodological note explaining the methods of data collection and analysis used for this report.

Global trafficking patterns

The analysis of global patterns of trafficking in persons contained in this report takes into account the age and gender of the detected victims, the gender and origin (local or foreign, relative to the country of prosecution) of traffickers and the relative prominence of the various forms of exploitation.

Victims

Between 2007 and 2010, women constituted the majority of victims of trafficking in persons detected globally. While the exact share of the total varies somewhat according to year, during the reporting period, between 55 and 60 per cent of the total number of detected victims were women.

Even though women comprise the majority of trafficking victims globally, their share of the total decreased somewhat during the reporting period. Over the period 2003-2006, more than two in three detected victims were women, as reported in the previous *Global Report on Trafficking in Persons* published in 2009. However, the total share of females of all ages among trafficked persons has not changed dramatically, as the decrease in the number of women victims detected was partially offset by the

---

1   See www.unodc.org/unodc/en/human-trafficking-fund/human-trafficking-fund.html.

FIG. 1: **Gender and age profile of victims detected globally, 2009**

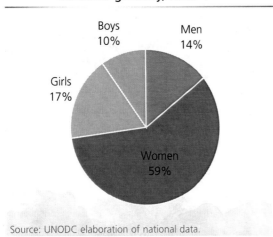

Source: UNODC elaboration of national data.

The trafficking of children appears to be increasing. Of the detected victims whose age profile was known and reported in the period 2007-2010, some 27 per cent were children. To compare, in the period 2003-2006, about 20 per cent were children. However, this trend was not homogenous at the global level. Many countries reported a marked increase in the share of detected cases of child trafficking between 2003 and 2010, whereas others reported no increase or a decrease in cases. Among the child victims, there were more detected cases of trafficking of girls than of boys: two of every three trafficked children were girls.

From region to region, there are significant differences in the gender/age profile of detected victims. While European and Central Asian countries report that 16 per cent of detected victims are children, in Africa and the Middle East approximately 68 per cent were children.

Traffickers

Information from more than 50 countries shows that of persons prosecuted for and/or convicted of trafficking in persons in the period 2007-2010, roughly two thirds are men. That proportion is nearly identical for prosecutions and convictions. These findings are similar to what was reported in the 2009 *Global Report on Trafficking in Persons.*

Although the majority of trafficking offenders are men,

increasing number of girl victims. The number of trafficked girls detected increased through the period 2007-2010, during which time girls constituted 15-20 per cent of the total number of detected victims.

During the same period, the number of trafficked men remained stable or increased slightly: 14-18 per cent of detected trafficking victims were men. The number of boys trafficked was relatively stable over the reporting period. Boys comprised 8-10 per cent of the total number of detected victims.

FIG. 2: **Share of child victims detected by region, 2007-2010**

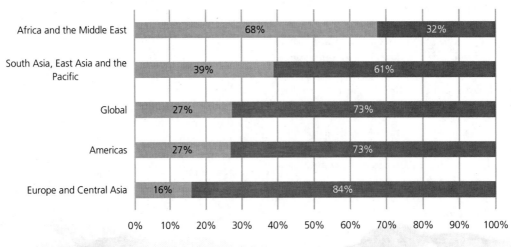

Source: UNODC elaboration of national data.

FIG. 3: **Shares of persons convicted of trafficking in persons, by gender, regional/subregional averages, 2007-2010**

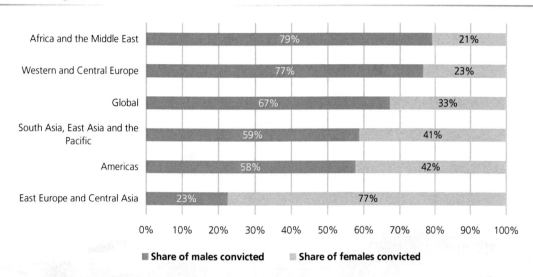

■ **Share of males convicted**   ■ **Share of females convicted**

Source: UNODC elaboration of national data.

the participation of women is higher for this crime than for most other crimes. Most countries report overall female offending rates below 15 per cent of the total for all crimes, with an average of some 12 per cent; while 30 per cent of trafficking in persons prosecutions and convictions are of women offenders. Statistical analyses show that the involvement of women in trafficking is more frequent in the trafficking of girls. Qualitative studies suggest that women involved in human trafficking are normally found in low-ranking positions of the trafficking networks and carry out duties that are more exposed to the risk of detection and prosecution than those of male traffickers.

There are clear regional and subregional differences regarding the involvement of women in trafficking in persons. In Eastern Europe and Central Asia, more than three fourths of those convicted of trafficking in persons offences are women. Although female conviction rates are also relatively high in Asia (although well below 50 per cent), the very high rate in Eastern Europe and Central Asia is exceptional.

With regard to the nationalities of those convicted of human trafficking, local nationals (from the perspective of the country of prosecution) comprised the vast majority of perpetrators. Although there were significant differences from country to country, foreign nationals constituted approximately one quarter of those convicted. That rate of foreign offenders is higher than for most other crimes.

There are large differences between regions and subregions. Compared with the rest of the world, countries in Europe and the Middle East report more foreign nationals among the detected offenders. Countries within the same region may also register differences according to the role of the country in the trafficking flow, as destination countries generally report a larger share of foreign nationals among the persons convicted of trafficking in persons than do source countries.

Forms of exploitation

Among the regions considered in this report, Africa and the Middle East, as well as South and East Asia and the Pacific, detect more cases of forced labour compared to other forms of exploitation. More cases of sexual exploitation than forced labour were detected in the Americas and Europe and Central Asia. Among all detected cases worldwide, trafficking in persons for sexual exploitation is more frequent than trafficking for forced labour. That statistic is likely to be biased, however, as European countries detect more victims than do any other region. Thus, exploitation patterns prominent in Europe may be disproportionately reflected in global totals. This means that the global proportion of trafficking for purposes of forced labour reported in the present report (36 per cent) is likely underestimated.

Among the detected forms of exploitation, forced labour is increasing rapidly. This may be due to improvements

FIG. 4: **Forms of exploitation, shares of the total number of detected victims, by region, 2007-2010**

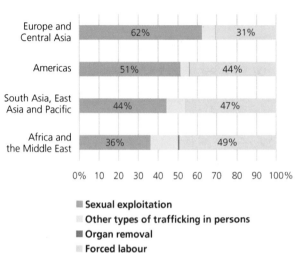

Source: UNODC elaboration of national data.

in many countries' capacities to detect trafficking for forced labour and to legislative enhancements adopted to ensure that this type of trafficking is covered by law. Compared with the 18-per-cent share reported for the period 2003-2006, detections of trafficking for forced labour doubled, reaching 36 per cent in the period 2007-2010.

Detections of other forms of trafficking remain relatively rare. Trafficking for the removal of organs, for example, comprised 0.2 per cent of the total number of detected cases in 2010. While this constitutes only a fraction of all cases, the geographical spread of those detected cases is significant: cases of trafficking for purposes of organ removal were reported by 16 countries in all regions considered in this report. Trafficking for purposes not specifically mentioned in the Trafficking in Persons Protocol, including begging, forced marriages, illegal adoption, participation in armed combat and the commission of crime (usually petty crime/street crime), accounted for 6 per cent of the total number of detected cases in 2010, including the 1.5 per cent of victims who were exploited for begging. The data reflect the wide variety of types of trafficking (domestic, intraregional and interregional) as well as forms of exploitation that in some cases have clear geographical connections, as in the case of trafficking of children on the African continent to be used as child soldiers and for rituals, a few cases of which have also been recorded in other regions.

Global trafficking flows

Trafficking in persons is a global crime affecting nearly all countries in every region of the world. Between 2007 and 2010, victims of 136 different nationalities were detected in 118 countries across the world, and most countries were affected by several trafficking flows. About 460 distinct trafficking flows around the world were identified during the reporting period.

Most of the trafficking flows are intraregional (i.e. trafficking within a region), with almost half of detected victims being trafficked from a country in the same region as the country of destination. Nearly one fourth of victims were trafficked between regions, and some 27 per cent of victims were trafficked domestically (i.e. within their country of origin).

Geographical distance between source and destination countries plays a role in the severity of the trafficking flows, as do economic differences. In general, victims are trafficked from relatively poorer areas to more affluent areas. That broad pattern can be found in many regions and subregions worldwide. However, most countries do not function solely as a country of origin or destination country for trafficking in persons but as a mixture of both roles.

Trafficking flows at destination

As stated above, nearly half of all trafficking is intraregional. More than 75 per cent of the trafficking flows considered are either short or medium range. This may be explained largely in terms of convenience and risk minimization for the traffickers, because shorter distances make it easier to manage the trafficking process.

From the vantage point of trafficking destinations, this means that the bulk of trafficking victims are trafficked within the region of origin. This is true for all regions and nearly all subregions. Countries in South and East Asia and the Pacific, as well as in Africa and in Eastern Europe and Central Asia, detect almost exclusively victims from within the region (including domestic trafficking), whereas several countries in the Middle East, North America and Western and Central Europe have a relatively high proportion of victims from other regions or subregions.

Countries of Western and Central Europe reported the greatest variety of origins and the greatest distances spanned by trafficking flows. During the reporting period, victims detected in those two subregions were of 112 different nationalities, from all regions of the world. Nevertheless, 64 per cent of the victims were trafficked from Western and Central European countries.

FIG. 5:   **Distribution of domestic, regional and transregional flows, as share of the total number of trafficking flows, 2007-2010**

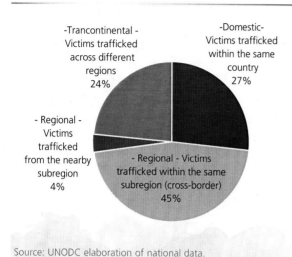

-Trancontinental -
Victims trafficked
across different
regions
24%

-Domestic-
Victims trafficked
within the same
country
27%

- Regional -
Victims
trafficked
from the nearby
subregion
4%

- Regional - Victims
trafficked within the same
subregion (cross-border)
45%

Source: UNODC elaboration of national data.

In North America, the situation is broadly similar: one third of detected victims come from outside the region, while a large majority of the victims are trafficked from North America, Central America and the Caribbean.

The Middle East is the part of the world where long-distance trafficking is most prominent, as about 70 per cent of the victims detected in the subregion come from other regions. In the Middle East between 2007 and 2010, victims of about 40 different nationalities were detected, including nationals of about 20 countries outside Africa and the Middle East (mainly Asians and Europeans).

Trafficking flows at origin

With respect to the countries of origin of human trafficking victims, there are also significant regional differences. Nationals of Western and Central European countries are almost exclusively detected in Europe. Similarly, victims from North America, Central America and the Caribbean and North Africa and the Middle East were not frequently detected outside their region of origin.

East Asians, South Asians, South Americans, sub-Saharan Africans and Eastern Europeans, meanwhile, were detected in many countries outside their region of origins. However, there are significant differences between those flows in terms of the volume of the flows and the geographical diffusion. The trafficking of sub-Saharan Africans, for example, is intense in Africa and the Middle East, as well

as Western Europe, but it is largely confined to those destinations.

South American and Eastern European victims are detected in a variety of countries in different regions and subregions, including the Middle East, East Asia, Europe and the Americas. However, these victims are detected in limited numbers outside their region of origin.

East Asian victims are detected in relatively large numbers in many countries across the world, making the flow from East Asia the most prominent transnational trafficking flow worldwide.

Domestic trafficking

Domestic trafficking accounted for more than 25 per cent of the total number of victims detected globally, and such trafficking has been reported by more than 60 of the 83 countries providing information on the nationality of victims. An increasing number of cases of domestic trafficking have been detected and reported in recent years. The percentage of human trafficking cases that were domestic trafficking cases rose from 19 per cent in 2007 to 31 per cent in 2010.

Regional patterns and flows

Europe and Central Asia

A large proportion of the victims of trafficking detected in Europe and Central Asia were women, while child trafficking victims accounted for about 16 per cent of the total. The detection of child trafficking increased somewhat during the reporting period. The most commonly detected type of trafficking was trafficking for purposes of sexual exploitation.

The most common origin of victims of cross-border trafficking in Western and Central Europe is the Balkans: 30 per cent of victims of cross-border trafficking are nationals from that area. Other significant origins for trafficking in Western and Central Europe are West Africa (14 per cent of total victims), East Asia (7 per cent), the Americas (7 per cent), Central Europe (7 per cent) and Eastern Europe and Central Asia (5 per cent). Domestic trafficking accounts for about one fourth of the victims detected.

Victims detected in Eastern European and Central Asian countries were almost exclusively from that same subregion. Victims from Eastern Europe and Central Asia were also detected in Western Europe and the Middle East. There are indications that trafficking of victims from Eastern Europe and Central Asia to other parts of the world is decreasing.

Americas

Most victims detected in the Americas are female. Children account for about 27 per cent of detected trafficking victims in the region. Forced labour is common in the Americas, accounting for 44 per cent of cases of detected victims. Sexual exploitation was involved in slightly more than half of detected cases.

Most trafficking flows involving countries in the Americas remain within the region. During the years considered, authorities in countries of North and Central America mainly detected victims from North and Central America who had been trafficked either within the country or across borders. Similarly, victims detected in South American countries mainly originated in the same country or another country of the subregion.

In terms of interregional flows, victims from South and East Asia were widely detected across the Americas, accounting for about 28 per cent of victims in North America, Central America and the Caribbean and about 10 per cent in South America. Victims originating in the Americas, in particular South America, Central America and the Caribbean, were detected in significant numbers in Western and Central Europe.

South Asia, East Asia and the Pacific

The majority of the victims detected in South and East Asia and the Pacific were female, and there is a comparatively high rate of women convicted for trafficking in persons offences in that region, where exploitation for forced labour is more common (47 per cent of victims) than sexual exploitation (44 per cent) and exploitation for domestic servitude is frequently reported.

While most of the trafficking flows affecting South and East Asia and the Pacific remain within the region (including those within a single country), the region is also a significant area of origin of interregional trafficking. East Asians were detected in 64 countries worldwide, often in relatively large numbers. South Asian victims were also detected in a broad range of destination countries.

Africa and the Middle East

Some two thirds of the victims detected in Africa and the Middle East were children. Almost half of the victims were exploited in forced labour, and 36 per cent of victims were trafficked for sexual exploitation. Other forms of trafficking, including for use as child soldiers, for rituals and for other purposes, accounted for 14 per cent of cases in the region.

There are significant differences between the subregions in terms of trafficking flows. The Middle East is primarily an area of destination for trafficking victims, particularly for East Asians, who constituted 35 per cent of the victims detected in the Middle East during the reporting period, and for South Asians (23 per cent of victims). The other significant areas of origin of victims detected in the Middle East are sub-Saharan Africa (20 per cent) and Eastern Europe and Central Asia (10 per cent).

Most of the victims detected in sub-Saharan Africa are trafficked within the country of origin or within the subregion. Trafficking of West African victims accounts for a significant share of trafficking in Europe, while East Africans constitute a significant portion of the victims detected in the Middle East.

The global criminal justice response

Much progress has been made in the fight against trafficking in persons, particularly since the entry into force of the Trafficking in Persons Protocol in 2003. One hundred and thirty-four countries and territories in the world have criminalized trafficking by establishing a specific offence, in line with the Protocol. Moreover, the number of countries still without an offence criminalizing trafficking in persons fell by more than half between 2008 and 2012.

Progress in convictions remains limited. Of the 132 countries covered in this report, 16 per cent did not record a single conviction for trafficking in persons between 2007 and 2010. However, more countries reported increases than reported decreases in the number of convictions between 2007 and 2010.

Significant challenges remain in the efforts to fully implement the United Nations Global Plan of Action to Combat Human Trafficking. Three areas stand out: knowledge and research, capacity-building and development, and monitoring and evaluation. Progress on those fronts will help the international community realize the ambitious goal set forth in the Global Plan of Action: to end the heinous crime of trafficking in persons.

INTRODUCTION
A STORY OF POWER AND VULNERABILITY

While many cases of trafficking in persons start as an attempt to improve the conditions of life, sometimes circumstances transform those attempts into incidences of exploitation and abuse. Deeply rooted social values and practices help create vulnerabilities that make victims of trafficking in persons (men, women and children) easy targets for criminals intent on profiting from those individuals' hopes of a better life. Recruiting and exploiting a vulnerable person is relatively easy and often carries a low risk of detection.

What makes people vulnerable, and who are some of the most vulnerable persons in a society? For one, children — both boys and girls — are clearly more vulnerable than adults, as they are neither mature enough nor legally empowered to make their own life decisions. They are dependent on guardians who may not always have their best interest at heart. Children, as a result of their lack of experience, are also prone to trusting others easily, which can be used by criminals to exploit them.

Additionally, in many societies, women are less empowered than men. This is true in terms of gender inequality in access to education and work opportunities and access to a fair and timely justice system, as well as attainment of human and social rights.[1] At the same time — and perhaps more significantly in terms of risk of becoming a victim of traffickers — this is also true in terms of physical strength, which makes females more vulnerable than males to exploitation through use of force or threats.

Another vulnerable group is would-be migrants, who are looking for opportunities abroad, or newly arrived immigrants, who are often without close family, friends or other support networks. Would-be migrants may be too eager to find opportunities abroad to critically assess job advertisements or recruiting firms. Newly arrived immigrants are often under pressure to find work quickly, which may make them more vulnerable to accepting dangerous job offers. Moreover, the irregular migration status of some migrants in their country of destination aggravates their vulnerability, as they are often afraid or reluctant to contact local authorities. Also, movement — particularly when it involves the crossing of borders — can create vulnerability to trafficking when those with restricted access to destination countries seek help from traffickers to cross borders with fraudulent documents or through other dishonest measures.

There are many other potentially vulnerable persons, including adolescents, who may become easy targets for exploitation in the sex industry, as seen with the phenomenon of "loverboys" in Europe. Persons with disabilities may be particularly vulnerable to being trafficked (often for begging), as may be albinos in some rural African communities, refugees fleeing wars or natural disasters and many other persons.

Gender, age, migration status, ethno-linguistic background and poverty (see the textbox on economics and trafficking on page 44) are by themselves insufficient explanations of vulnerability, but they tend to become factors of vulnerability if they provide grounds for discrimination from the rest of the community. While anyone could become a trafficking victim, persons who lack protection, who are not integrated in the surrounding community and who are isolated by the national authorities or by the societies where they live are at greater risk of human trafficking. In these areas of discrimination and marginalization, traffickers find the space to exploit the vulnerable situation of potential victims.

On the other hand, the powers of traffickers are based on financial and social resources that can be used for profit-making. These resources may have originated from diverse criminal activities or from business and social networks used for criminal purposes. Business networks can include relationships with individuals who have the means to recruit people, such as owners of recruitment agencies, or means to transport people, such as truck or taxi drivers, the ability to assist with travel documents, such as embassy personnel, or the possibility to abuse the services of trafficked persons, such as restaurant or brothel owners. Social networks can include relationships with certain ethnic or family groups or other distinct groups. With the financial resources and social networks, the traffickers can create those powers that are needed to organize the trafficking in persons crime.

Human trafficking patterns by and large mirror these powers and vulnerabilities, both in terms of the criminals and the victims. The most common trafficker profile is a male who is a national of the country where the exploita-

1   See, for example, UN-Women, *Progress of the World's Women 2011-2012: In Pursuit of Justice*.

tion takes place, whereas most victims are women and children, usually foreign and often from backgrounds characterized by economic deprivation and/or lack of decent employment opportunities.

The vulnerabilities can also help explain the prominence of some types of human trafficking flows. Within any given country, people from particular areas may be detected as victims of trafficking in persons more frequently than people from other locations. For example, some countries experience high levels of trafficking movements from rural to urban areas, as a result of the greater range of available employment options and relatively greater affluence found in most large cities. At the regional (or subregional) level, patterns of trafficking from poorer towards richer countries and/or areas can often be discerned.

What is trafficking in persons?

According to the United Nations definition,[2] human trafficking can be understood as a process by which people are recruited in their community and exploited by traffickers using deception and/or some form of coercion to lure and control them. There are three distinct elements of this crime: the act, the means and the purpose. All three elements must be present to constitute a trafficking in persons offence, although each element has a range of manifestations.

Broadly speaking, "the act" means the recruitment, transport, harbouring or receipt of persons intended for trafficking, whereas "the means" refers to the threat or use of force, deception, coercion or abuse of power used to lure the victims. "The purpose" is the form of exploitation to which the traffickers subject their victims, whether sexual exploitation, forced labour, domestic servitude or one of a range of other forms.

One of the characteristics of trafficking in persons is that it was criminalized only relatively recently. Although the

••
2   The Protocol to Prevent, Suppress and Punish Trafficking in Persons, Especially Women and Children, supplementing the United Nations Convention against Transnational Organized Crime (hereafter referred to as the "Trafficking in Persons Protocol"), defines trafficking in persons as follows: "the recruitment, transportation, transfer, harbouring or receipt of persons, by means of the threat or use of force or other forms of coercion, of abduction, of fraud, of deception, of the abuse of power or of a position of vulnerability or of the giving or receiving of payments or benefits to achieve the consent of a person having control over another person, for the purpose of exploitation. Exploitation shall include, at a minimum, the exploitation of the prostitution of others or other forms of sexual exploitation, forced labour or services, slavery or practices similar to slavery, servitude or the removal of organs."

exploitation of others has always taken place, trafficking in persons, as understood today, has been defined specifically at the international level (in the United Nations Trafficking in Persons Protocol) only since the early 2000s. Some countries have yet to implement legislation addressing the problem. This means that the awareness of and capacity to tackle trafficking in persons is often lower than for other, more "established" crimes.

Trafficking in persons is also a *global* crime affecting nearly every country in the world. As a result, there are vast numbers of local, national and regional interpretations and responses to this crime, and an immense number of stakeholders involved in efforts to tackle it. Moreover, the present report has identified a large number of trafficking in persons flows across the world, which illustrates the global scope of the crime. As defined, a trafficking flow is a link between two countries or two places within the same country (one of origin and one of destination for victims of trafficking in persons), with at least five officially detected victims having been trafficked from the origin to the destination country: there are about 460 such flows across all regions and subregions, and involving most countries.

Moreover, trafficking in persons is a *complex* crime that manifests itself in myriad ways across the world. Although all cases of trafficking in persons are defined by the presence of its three constituent elements — the act, means and purpose — the particulars of each case differ, often significantly. Popular representations of trafficking in persons as mainly concerning the trafficking of women for the sex industry may have reduced the appreciation of the complexity of the crime in some places, although in recent years, accounts of trafficking for forced labour and other forms of exploitation have become somewhat more prominent. This may help foster a more comprehensive understanding of this multifaceted crime.

As for all crimes, official statistics on trafficking in persons represent only the tip of the iceberg, as criminals generally go to great lengths to prevent the detection of their activities. This means that a large part of the phenomenon remains hidden. While the size of the iceberg will remain unknown, it is possible to obtain an understanding of its shape and characteristics by analysing the visible tip. Thus by using information concerning the cases officially detected by the national authorities, in conjunction with a rigorous analysis of the statistical bias affecting these cases, it will be possible to discern the main human trafficking patterns and flows. However, it will not be possible to draw solid conclusions regarding the dimension of the problem.

United Nations response to trafficking in persons

On 25 December 2003, the Protocol to Prevent, Suppress and Punish Trafficking in Persons, Especially Women and Children, supplementing the United Nations Convention against Transnational Organized Crime, entered into force. Trafficking in persons was thus clearly defined and recognized by the international community as a serious organized criminal activity. By ratifying the Protocol, States Members of the United Nations demonstrated their commitment to combating this crime. As of August 2012, 170 countries had ratified the Protocol.

In July 2010, the General Assembly marked another milestone in the multinational effort to combat human trafficking, by adopting the United Nations Global Plan of Action to Combat Trafficking in Persons. The Global Plan of Action lists a number of specific provisions to be adopted by the international community to promote universal ratification and to reinforce the implementation of the Protocol. For instance, the Global Plan of Action also prompted the creation of the United Nations Voluntary Trust Fund for Victims of Trafficking in Persons, Especially Women and Children.[3]

The Global Plan of Action also called for an increased knowledge base with regard to trafficking in persons, in order to facilitate the creation and implementation of evidence-based programmatic interventions. In paragraph 60 of the Plan of Action, UNODC is assigned the mandate and duty to collect relevant data and report on trafficking in persons patterns and flows at the national, regional and international levels:

> Request the Secretary-General, as a matter of priority, to strengthen the capacity of the United Nations Office on Drugs and Crime to collect information and report biennially, starting in 2012, on patterns and flows of trafficking in persons at the national, regional and international levels in a balanced, reliable and comprehensive manner, in close cooperation and collaboration with Member States, and share best practices and lessons learned from various initiatives and mechanisms. (Assembly resolution 64/293, para. 60).

3 See www.unodc.org/unodc/en/human-trafficking-fund/human-trafficking-fund.html.

This mandate was reiterated by the Commission on Crime Prevention and Criminal Justice in April 2011,[4] further affirming the intention of Member States to collaborate with UNODC for the production of more comprehensive assessments and systematic monitoring of trafficking in persons.

The Global Report on Trafficking in Persons 2012

The present report aims to enhance the current knowledge on trafficking in persons in its national and transnational manifestations. Such observation of trafficking trends can be comprehensively conducted only from an international standpoint. While national-level research may accurately present the human trafficking situation in a particular country and provide valuable input to international analyses, an international authority is well placed to discern commonalities and differences between countries or regions and identify trafficking flows and patterns in different parts of the world.

By monitoring the international dynamics of trafficking, it is possible to gain a broader understanding of the global trends in trafficking in persons. Are certain trafficking patterns mainly associated with some countries, or an entire region or a subregion? Are some forms of trafficking more prevalent in particular areas? Is trafficking from certain areas diminishing, increasing or in the process of being displaced?

Furthermore, developing a comprehensive global understanding of the problem may also assist national-level efforts. With increased knowledge about international trafficking patterns and flows, it is easier to understand — and with time, hopefully, even to predict — the trafficking characteristics at the national level. This knowledge can be generated only by collecting and synthesizing information concerning individual countries. The explanatory power of the present report therefore relies on the quantity and quality of the information provided by national institutions. This is why the collaboration with Member States is crucial for UNODC to fulfil the mandate assigned by the Global Plan of Action.

4 In its resolution 20/3, the Commission requested the United Nations Office on Drugs and Crime to strengthen its capacity to collect and analyse information and to report biennially, starting in 2012, on patterns, forms and flows of trafficking in persons at all levels in a reliable and comprehensive manner, with a balanced perspective on both supply and demand, as a step towards, inter alia, improving the implementation of the Trafficking in Persons Protocol, in close cooperation and collaboration with Member States, and to share best practices and lessons learned from various initiatives and mechanisms.

The previous *Global Report on Trafficking in Persons*[5] published in 2009 was a first global effort in collating official national-level information. This was done to assess the trafficking situation, particularly in terms of the criminal justice system response, at the national and international levels. This *Global Report* continues the work started earlier in terms of the methodological approach, paying particular attention to trafficking flows and patterns, as requested by the General Assembly.

Coverage and data collection

A report cannot be truly global if its data and analysis do not cover the situation in most of the world. At the same time, the study should be based on solid information provided by authoritative sources. Therefore, the collection of data was conducted with a dual objective in mind: achieving the broadest possible coverage, using the most solid source of information.

The vast majority of the data collected for this *Global Report on Trafficking in Persons* came from national institutions (88 per cent of the data series collected). Other sources of information were international governmental organizations (5 per cent of the data) and non-governmental organizations (7 per cent).

The information was collected by UNODC in three ways: through a short, dedicated questionnaire distributed to Governments;[6] by considering the relevant results of the regular United Nations Survey of Crime Trends and Operations of Criminal Justice Systems used to survey Member States on official statistics on different forms of crime;[7] and by collecting official information available in the public domain (national police reports, Ministry of Justice reports, national trafficking in persons reports etc.).[8] The

information that was collected was subsequently shared with the national authorities for verification.

The countries not covered by this report responded neither to the ad hoc questionnaire sent by UNODC to Member States nor to the crime trends survey. Furthermore, the UNODC research team was unable to find data for these countries corresponding to the indicators used for the present report that were published by a national authority and in the public domain.

Even when countries responded and provided data, not all the information could be systematically used. Some countries provided partial information or data in a non-standard format. All information collected and used in this report is presented in the country profiles, which also specify the information sources. Information for this edition of the *Global Report* was collected from 132 countries and territories. All world regions are more or less equally covered and the list of countries and the regional classification system used in this report can be found at the end of this introductory section.

The information collected concerned the number and the profile (age, gender and nationality) of the victims detected, as well as the number and profile (gender and nationality) of the persons prosecuted and convicted for trafficking in persons or related offences. Information was also collected about the countries of destination for victims repatriated to their own countries. In addition, information about the forms of exploitation used by traffickers were collected when available. The time period covered is 2007-2010, or to a more recent date, unless otherwise indicated.

The collection of data for this report took two years — from August 2010 to August 2012 — and information was gathered on approximately 55,000 victims and 50,000 offenders detected around the world. It was not always possible to obtain the profile of those individuals, usually owing to incomplete reporting at the country level. For that reason, the size of the sample forming the basis for the analysis varies according to the indicator in question. The data collection involved a research team at UNODC headquarters, as well as researchers in various UNODC field offices around the world.

5   Available at www.unodc.org/glotip.

6   Included in the information on methodology, available on the report's web page (www.unodc.org/glotip).

7   In its resolution 1984/48, the Economic and Social Council requested the Secretary-General to maintain and develop the United Nations crime-related database by continuing to conduct surveys of crime trends and the operations of criminal justice systems. The major goal of the United Nations Surveys of Crime Trends and Operations of Criminal Justice Systems is to collect data on the incidence of reported crime and the operations of criminal justice systems. The survey results provide an overview of trends and interrelationships between various parts of the criminal justice system to promote informed decision-making in administration, nationally and internationally (available at www.unodc.org/unodc/en/data-and-analysis/United-Nations-Surveys-on-Crime-Trends-and-the-Operations-of-Criminal-Justice-Systems.html).

8   About 66 per cent of the information that forms the basis of this report was collected through a dedicated questionnaire sent to Governments, while about 3 per cent of the data series was collected through the United Nations Survey of Crime Trends and Operations

of Criminal Justice Systems, and the remaining 31 per cent was proactively collected by the UNODC team by screening the public domain.

Strengths and weaknesses of the report

The characteristics of trafficking in persons described above all present distinct challenges to the making of a global research report. The fact that in many countries the criminal offences criminalizing trafficking in persons are of recent date means that there is a limited set of official data and previous research to draw upon. Its global nature translates into a large number of national legislative and enforcement contexts to navigate, synthesize and represent. The complexity of human trafficking requires a thorough understanding of the crime's many manifestations and rapidly changing nature.

The guiding principles behind this report are to use solid numbers and clear sources. Limiting the underlying data set to officially detected victims and offenders of trafficking in persons, as has been done for this report, has important advantages. It is a factual approach, based on objective elements: a large number of detected cases and verified data. Patterns and flows of detected cases of trafficking in persons have been derived on the basis of the number of cases detected by national authorities. The report contains the authors' assessment of whether these cases are more or less representative of the whole trafficking phenomenon and how this information should be interpreted. Ultimately, this assessment is left to the reader. Data are presented transparently, with acknowledgement of the sources.

Moreover, given the recent prioritization of human trafficking in several countries, the knowledge base available to researchers is increasing. More countries are making efforts to tackle this crime, and as a result, more countries have information to share. The number of victims officially detected is now large enough to yield a reasonably detailed sketch of the profile of the victims, and although information on traffickers is more scarce, it is possible to identify some common characteristics. To ensure transparency, the major sections of the report contain an indication of the sample size underlying the analysis (i.e. the number of detected cases the results were derived from).

Finally, the data collection for the *Global Report on Trafficking in Persons* of 2009 — which was also based on official information — yielded data on some of the indicators used in the present report. This means that some trends can be ascertained for countries and regions with sufficient and solid data, particularly in relation to human trafficking flows.

This approach of employing officially reported data nearly exclusively also necessarily introduces some biases. It

should be kept in mind that official data are not collected for research but for administrative purposes to record the enforcement efforts in relation to particular legislation. The reliance on criminal justice response data means that one key bias is related to the likelihood that criminal justice systems may detect and report certain forms of trafficking more than others. One example is the likely overrepresentation of trafficking for sexual exploitation in this report. Trafficking for sexual exploitation has for some time been the primary focus of much anti-trafficking work, a situation which has likely influenced legislative and enforcement efforts. As a result, the official reports on which this report is based may overestimate trafficking for sexual exploitation and, as a result, trafficking of women, because women represent the overwhelming majority of victims of trafficking for sexual exploitation.

Conversely, data on officially detected victims is likely to underrepresent the prevalence of trafficking for forced labour, as this form of trafficking in persons has received less emphasis than that of sexual exploitation. The picture may be changing, however. The global trend observed is an increase in the proportion of detected trafficking cases that are for the purpose of forced labour, which may mean that the gap between the number of trafficking in persons cases detected globally and the real dimensions of the problem of trafficking in persons is narrowing.

Another important bias is related to the availability of data, which varies considerably from region to region, in spite of the fact that all regions have reached a critical mass of reporting countries. As a result of the uneven reporting levels, results for some regions are more reliable than for others. For example, the regional analyses for Africa are based on weaker data than those for Europe or the Americas. The weaknesses are due to lower levels of reporting from African countries, as well as the lower detection rates. As a consequence of this geographical detection bias, the global results on patterns and flows tend to reflect the patterns and flows of Europe and the Americas to a greater degree than those of Africa and Asia. This should be kept in mind when considering the global analysis.

Organization of the report

This report is divided into three main chapters. Chapter I provides a global overview of the patterns and flows of trafficking in persons. The data collected at the global level reveals the profile of the victims detected and how that profile has changed over the period considered. The chapter presents the forms of exploitation reported globally, with insight into emerging forms of exploitation that are less frequently reported. The chapter also presents global patterns concerning the profile of the offenders and analyses the global flows on the basis of the nationality of the victims detected, as well as the countries of repatriation of nationals trafficked abroad. This analysis yields a global overview of the intensity, diffusion and range of the major human trafficking flows detected and reported.

Chapter II analyses patterns and flows of trafficking in persons at the regional level. The 132 countries covered have been categorized into four regions: Europe and Central Asia, the Americas, South and East Asia and the Pacific, and Africa and the Middle East. The order of presentation is based on the size of the sample used for the analysis in each region, with Europe and Central Asia having the highest number of victims detected during the period considered. The regional groupings are then divided into subregions, when doing so helps facilitate further analysis (Western and Central Europe, Eastern Europe and Central Asia, North and Central America and the Caribbean, South America, South Asia, East Asia and the Pacific, North Africa and the Middle East and sub-Saharan Africa). The categorization of countries and

regions is based on criteria of geographical proximity, socioeconomic commonalities and institutional linkages.

The Global Plan of Action also requested UNODC to share best practices and lessons learned in the area of trafficking in persons. Chapter III presents such information as it relates to legislation and criminal justice. First, the status of the international legal framework, including multilateral instruments, are described. Secondly, an analysis is given of the responses by countries to trafficking in persons, on the basis of information on national legislation and trends in prosecutions and convictions.

Additional, related material is available on the Global Report website (www.unodc.org/glotip), including the country profiles, which contain country-level information for the countries covered in the report. Each profile contains information on trafficking patterns and flows in the country concerned. All country profiles are introduced by a brief description of the current legislative framework of the country, which is needed to accurately interpret official statistics.

The questionnaire used to collect the data is also available online (www.unodc.org/glotip).

MAP 1:   **Countries covered by the data collection for this report**

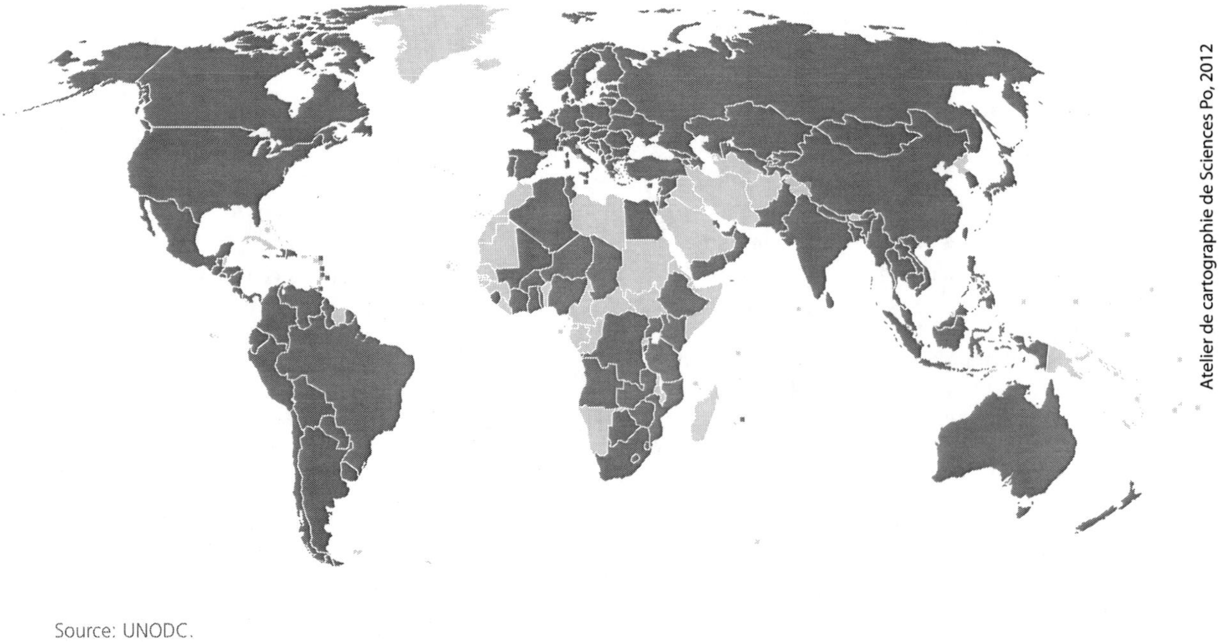

Atelier de cartographie de Sciences Po, 2012

Source: UNODC.

TABLE 1: Countries covered by the report, by region and subregion

AFRICA AND THE MIDDLE EAST 36 STATES (on the total 66 UN Member States in the region)		AMERICAS 28 STATES (on the total 35 UN Member States in the region)		EUROPE AND CENTRAL ASIA 48 STATES (on the total 53 UN Member States in the region)		SOUTH ASIA, EAST ASIA AND THE PACIFIC 20 STATES (on the total 39 UN Member States in the region)	
North Africa and the Middle East (total: 12)	Sub-Saharan Africa (total: 24)	North and Central America and the Caribbean (total: 17)	South America (total: 11)	Western and Central Europe (total: 37)	Eastern Europe and Central Asia (total: 11)	South Asia (total: 5)	East Asia and the Pacific (total: 15)
Algeria	Angola	Barbados	Argentina	Albania	Armenia	Bangladesh	Australia
Bahrain	Botswana	Canada	Bolivia (Plurinational State of)	Austria	Azerbaijan	India	Cambodia
Egypt	Burkina Faso	Costa Rica	Brazil	Belgium	Belarus	Nepal	China
Israel	Burundi	Dominican Republic	Chile	Bosnia and Herzegovina	Georgia	Pakistan	Indonesia
Jordan	Chad	El Salvador	Colombia	Bulgaria	Kazakhstan	Sri Lanka	Japan
Lebanon	Côte d'Ivoire	Guatemala	Ecuador	Croatia	Kyrgyzstan		Lao People's Democratic Republic
Oman	Democratic Republic of the Congo	Haiti	Guyana	Cyprus	Republic of Moldova		Malaysia
Qatar	Ethiopia	Honduras	Paraguay	Czech Republic	Russian Federation		Mongolia
Syrian Arab Republic	Ghana	Jamaica	Peru	Denmark	Tajikistan		Myanmar
Tunisia	Kenya	Mexico	Uruguay	Estonia	Ukraine		New Zealand
United Arab Emirates	Lesotho	Nicaragua	Venezuela (Bolivarian Republic of)	Finland	Uzbekistan		Philippines
Yemen	Mali	Panama		France			Republic of Korea
	Mauritius	Saint Kitts and Nevis		Germany			Singapore
	Mozambique	Saint Lucia		Greece			Thailand
	Niger	Saint Vincent and the Grenadines		Hungary			Viet Nam
	Nigeria	Trinidad and Tobago		Ireland			
	Sierra Leone	United States of America		Italy			
	South Africa			Latvia			

AFRICA AND THE MIDDLE EAST 36 STATES (on the total 66 UN Member States in the region)		AMERICAS 28 STATES (on the total 35 UN Member States in the region)		EUROPE AND CENTRAL ASIA 48 STATES (on the total 53 UN Member States in the region)		SOUTH ASIA, EAST ASIA AND THE PACIFIC 20 STATES (on the total 39 UN Member States in the region)	
North Africa and the Middle East (total: 12)	Sub-Saharan Africa (total: 24)	North and Central America and the Caribbean (total: 17)	South America (total: 11)	Western and Central Europe (total: 37)	Eastern Europe and Central Asia (total: 11)	South Asia (total: 5)	East Asia and the Pacific (total: 15)
	Swaziland			Lithuania			
	Togo			Luxembourg			
	Uganda			Malta			
	United Republic of Tanzania			Monaco			
	Zambia			Montenegro			
	Zimbabwe			Netherlands			
				Norway			
				Poland			
				Portugal			
				Romania			
				Serbia			
				Slovakia			
				Slovenia			
				Spain			
				Sweden			
				Switzerland			
				The former Yugoslav Republic of Macedonia			
				Turkey			
				United Kingdom of Great Britain and Northern Ireland			

MAP 2:   **Regional and subregional designations used in this report**

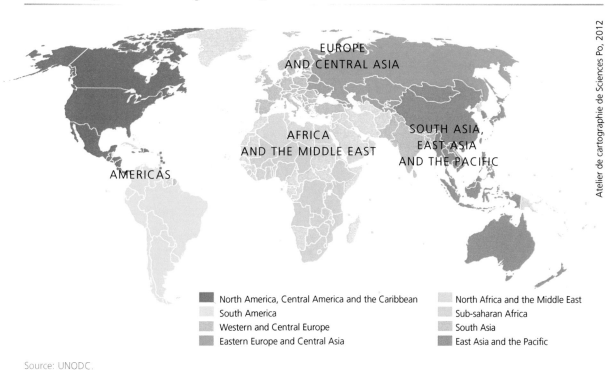

EUROPE
AND CENTRAL ASIA

AFRICA
AND THE MIDDLE EAST

SOUTH ASIA,
EAST ASIA
AND THE PACIFIC

AMERICAS

Atelier de cartographie de Sciences Po, 2012

- North America, Central America and the Caribbean
- South America
- Western and Central Europe
- Eastern Europe and Central Asia
- North Africa and the Middle East
- Sub-saharan Africa
- South Asia
- East Asia and the Pacific

Source: UNODC.

CHAPTER I
PATTERNS AND FLOWS OF
TRAFFICKING IN PERSONS:
GLOBAL OVERVIEW

In the United Nations Global Plan of Action to Combat Trafficking in Persons, Member States requested for the present report to focus on patterns and flows of trafficking in persons. As a result, much of the data collection was oriented towards enabling such an emphasis. Most of the indicators that Governments were asked to report on concerned trafficking patterns and flows, and chapter I presents a global overview of the findings.

A. TRAFFICKING PATTERNS: VICTIMS, TRAFFICKERS AND FORMS OF EXPLOITATION

By "patterns" of trafficking in persons, this report means basic profile information such as the age and gender of victims and traffickers and the forms of exploitation used by traffickers. Many countries were able to provide information on the age and gender of detected victims, as well as on the gender of prosecuted and/or convicted traffickers. Most countries also supplied a breakdown of the types of exploitation to which the detected victims of trafficking in persons in their country were subjected — in most cases either sexual exploitation or forced labour, with generally limited reports of other forms of exploitation.

1. Victims: becoming vulnerable

There is a common perception that women and children are more vulnerable than adult men to becoming victims of trafficking in persons. This perception is reflected in the full name of the Protocol to Prevent, Suppress and Punish Trafficking in Persons, Especially Women and Children, which singles out the trafficking of women and children as issues of particular concern.

An analysis of the data collected for this report, which covered the profiles of some 43,000 victims officially detected by national authorities worldwide between 2007 and 2010 or more recently, confirms the need for special attention to these two categories of victims. Women and children are the two most frequently reported groups of trafficked persons.

Most detected trafficking victims are female adults.

The age and gender profile was known and reported for about 29,000 victims detected globally between 2007 and 2010 or more recently. Almost 60 per cent of them were adult women. During the individual years of the reporting period, the share of women trafficked and detected ranged between 55 and 60 per cent of the total number of detected victims. Women comprise the bulk of victims detected globally, which suggests that being a woman in many parts of the world is connected to those vulnerabilities that lead to victimization through trafficking in persons.

More countries reported information on the age and gender of the detected victims for the year 2009.[1] An analysis of the data for 2009 confirms the age/gender patterns recorded during the whole reporting period. The data also indicate that the percentage of women among the total number of detected victims of trafficking globally is in the range of 60 per cent.

FIG. 6: **Gender and age profile of victims detected globally,** 2009

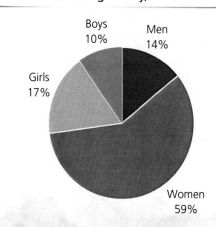

Source: UNODC elaboration of national data.

[1] For 2009, 65 countries reported the age and gender of about 6,900 detected victims. For the other years, the data were as follows: for 2007, 49 countries and about 6,000 victims; for 2008, 61 countries and about 6,200 victims; for 2010, 62 countries and 8,200 victims; and for 2011, 12 countries and 1,700 victims.

Taking into account the number of trafficking victims detected during the reporting period who were girls, the total proportion of female victims was 75 per cent of all victims. In particular, in 2009 the share of detected victims who were female was also about three quarters of all victims. The 2009 *Global Report on Trafficking in Persons*[2] reported slightly higher values for the period 2003-2006.

FIG. 7:   **Share of female victims detected globally, by age,** 2006 and 2009

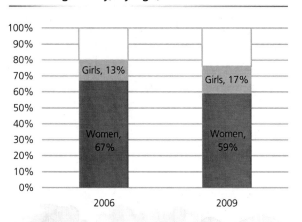

Source: UNODC/UN.GIFT for 2006; UNODC elaboration of national data for 2009.

The share of women and girls among detected victims over the past few years has been decreasing somewhat. In particular, in recent years there has been an evident reduction of the share of detected adult women, which has been partially offset by an increased share of girls among the detected victims of trafficking.

Nonetheless, trafficking in persons remains a crime with a strong gender connotation. Adult women represent the bulk of female victims. Trafficking of girls accounts for about 15-20 per cent of the total number of victims detected between 2007 and 2010 (or more recently), representing the second largest category of detected trafficking victims globally. As indicated above, this share has been increasing in recent years. This increase should be seen in the light of the overall increasing share of children among trafficked victims detected recently.

More than a quarter of the detected victims are children.

The age profile was known and reported for about 43,000 victims detected globally between 2007 and 2010. Some

2   UNODC/UN.GIFT (2009).

12,000 of those victims were children,[3] accounting for a total of 27 per cent of the victims. Among these, girls were more frequently detected than boys. On average, of every three trafficked children detected by the authorities, two were girls and one was a boy. Between 2007 and 2010, the share of boys among the total number of detected victims was in the range of 8-10 per cent, while girls accounted for about 15-20 per cent. That proportion remained constant throughout the reporting period.

This reinforces this crime's characteristics with respect to gender and emphasizes the circumstances creating vulnerabilities that push females to become victims of trafficking in persons.

When comparing the proportion of child trafficking detected between 2007 and 2010 (27 per cent), to the proportion recorded earlier between 2003 and 2006 (around 20 per cent), a general increase of detected child trafficking at the global level can be discerned. This finding is further corroborated by the fact that more than 20 countries recorded a clear increase in the proportion of child trafficking detected in the period 2007-2010 compared with the period 2003-2006. In recent years, the increase has been greater for girls: in 2006, 13 per cent of the total victims detected were girls; in 2009, 17 per cent were girls.

However, when considering the information presented in the more detailed regional analyses, it can be seen that the trend observed is not homogenous across all regions. The trend described above is more clearly noticeable in a number of countries in Europe and Central Asia, as well as in some countries in the Americas and in Asia.

The scale of child trafficking also varies greatly geographically, varying between regions, subregions and countries.

During the period 2007-2010, children accounted for about 16 per cent of the trafficking victims detected in Europe and Central Asia. The Americas recorded the proportion of child victims at some 27 per cent, which is in line with the global average. South and East Asia and the Pacific recorded a proportion higher than the global average: about 40 per cent of all victims detected between 2007 and 2010 were children. In Africa and the Middle East, children comprised a large majority of the victims reported.

3   As defined in article 3 (d) of the Trafficking in Persons Protocol, the term "child" as used in this report means any person under 18 years of age.

FIG. 8: **Share of child victims detected, by region, 2007-2010**

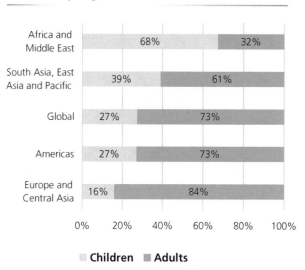

Source: UNODC elaboration of national data.

European countries have a comparatively greater capacity to detect and report on trafficking in persons, whereas African countries have a lesser capacity. As a result, global statistics tend to reflect European patterns disproportionately compared with patterns in Africa. Trafficking in persons in Africa is characterized by a high proportion of child victims. Conversely, countries in Europe record a limited share of child victims.

The aggregated values tend to obscure important differences at the local level. Child trafficking appears to be less frequent than adult trafficking when values are compared at the global level. However, when the regional- and country-level data are considered, it is clear that during the reporting period, in many countries, children were more frequently detected as trafficking victims than were adults.

Map 3 shows that children were more frequently detected as victims of trafficking in persons on the African continent, in the Andean countries, in South-East Asia and in the Western Balkans.

Men are also targeted.

Trafficking of adult men appears to be less common than trafficking in women or children. Nevertheless, men may become vulnerable to trafficking in certain circumstances, for example, if they have a minority ethno-linguistic background or a low socioeconomic standing in their own country, or they may be vulnerable owing to a lack of legal status abroad.

The proportion of total victims detected globally who are men is not insignificant. Between 2007 and 2010 or more recently, national authorities detected more than 4,500 adult male victims of trafficking in persons. Men represent about 15 per cent of the victims detected globally over the reporting period. Similar percentages were recorded during the 2003-2006 period, which indicates that the global

MAP 3: **Share of children among the total number of victims detected, by country, 2007-2010**

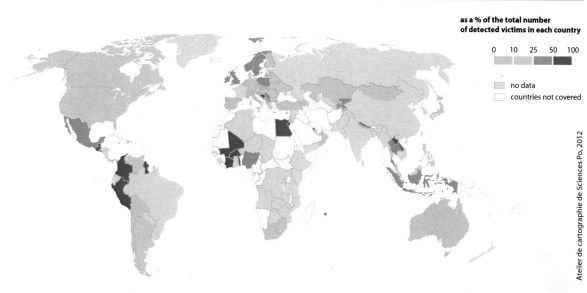

Source: UNODC elaboration of national data.

FIG. 9: **Share of male victims detected globally,** by age, 2006 and 2009

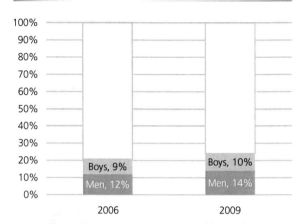

Source: UNODC/UN.GIFT for 2006; UNODC elaboration of national data for 2009.

FIG. 10: **Gender of persons prosecuted and convicted of trafficking in persons,** global average, 2007-2010

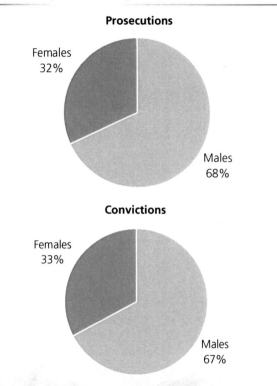

Source: UNODC elaboration of national data.

share of detected victims who were men remained relatively constant during the whole decade.

Europe and Central Asia and the Americas recorded higher shares of adult male victims compared with other regions. Of the limited information available on trafficking of males in Africa and the Middle East, most of it concerned the Middle East subregion. In Asia, the number of countries reporting adult males among victims is limited, and the share of men never rose above 10 per cent during the reporting period in the countries concerned.

As previously mentioned, official statistics stemming from law enforcement reporting may not always be representative of the human trafficking situation in each country. Enforcement efforts may emphasize certain manifestations of the crime, which could lead to overrepresentation or underrepresentation of some types of trafficking. From the currently available data, a very limited number of adult men were identified as victims of trafficking in persons — particularly in sub-Saharan Africa and in East Asia. This likely owes more to the limited detection capacity in those regions than to the lesser severity of this form of trafficking. More efforts are required to enhance knowledge and awareness about the trafficking of men.

2. Traffickers: abusing their power

In contrast to the vulnerability of victims is the power that the traffickers possess enabling them to commit a trafficking crime. While most of the victims of trafficking are females, children and/or migrants, the vast majority of the detected offenders implicated in trafficking in persons are men and nationals of the country where the crime is committed. However, the exact proportions of this male and "own nationals" involvement vary between the countries and regions.

Based on information provided by 51 countries regarding the gender of people prosecuted for trafficking in persons, as well as data from 56 countries regarding the gender of those convicted between 2007 and 2010, males comprise some two thirds of those involved in the trafficking process.[4] There is no significant gender profile distinction between those prosecuted and convicted. These findings are similar to those presented in the *Global Report on Trafficking in Persons* of 2009.[5]

4   Between 2007 and 2010 (or more recently), 51 countries reported on almost 12,000 persons prosecuted for trafficking in persons. Of them, 3,800 were female and 8,100 were male. During the same period, 56 countries reported on more than 10,000 persons convicted for trafficking in persons: 7,000 were male and 3,300 were female.

5   UNODC/UN.GIFT (2009), pp. 45-47.

FIG. 11:   **Proportion of offenders convicted of all crimes who are women, selected countries, 2006-2009**

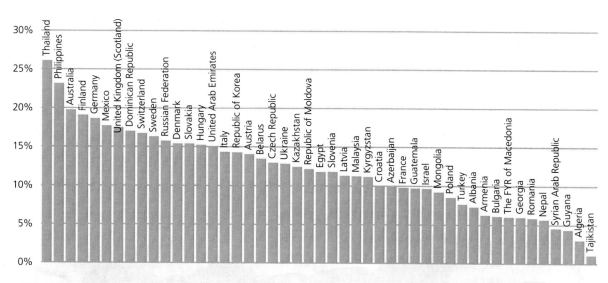

Source: UNODC, United Nations Survey of Crime Trends and Operations of Criminal Justice Systems.

In comparison, data collected through the United Nations Survey of Crime Trends and Operations of Criminal Justice Systems on convictions for all crimes in 66 countries during the period 2006-2009 reveals that most countries reported female offending rates below 15 per cent. The average share is some 12 per cent, with only a few countries reporting shares above 20 per cent.

Although a clear majority of those prosecuted/convicted for trafficking in persons are men, trafficking in persons is a crime with a relatively high rate of female involvement. In fact, the relative prominence of female offending rates related to trafficking in persons is a clear exception in the criminological taxonomy. Few other crimes record this level of female participation.

This high rate of involvement by women in trafficking in persons deserves closer attention. It is not surprising that a crime for which 75-80 per cent of detected victims are female also involves a higher rate of female offenders. As a matter of fact, the data show that there may be a link between the profile of the victims and that of the offenders. In particular, there is a positive correlation between the share of girls detected as victims and the share of women convicted for trafficking in persons.[6] Countries that detect

a relatively high percentage of girl victims also have higher rates of women convicted of trafficking in persons. Conversely, in countries where fewer girls are among the victims, fewer women are convicted of the crime. This suggests that women traffickers are relatively likely to participate in forms of trafficking related to the exploitation of girls, in relation to whom adult women could have power to leverage.

This quantitative result provides support to the hypothesis that female offending is particularly connected to sexual exploitation, which has been noted in a number of qualitative studies. Some of those studies indicated the emergence of women as traffickers in the late 1990s, and more recently in 2008.[7] A study conducted on Eastern European trafficking networks operating for sexual exploitation in Italy in the late 1990s showed that women were becoming more numerous among those convicted of trafficking in persons.

The study also showed that women are normally used for activities such as guarding the victims in the place where exploitation takes place, whether it is the street or a brothel, or receiving cash from the clients, as reflected in figure 13.

••

0,003. The correlation is conducted among the variables provided by the 33 countries that provided data on both variables.

••

6   A parametric correlation conducted on the percentage of the underage females on the total victims and the percentage of women convicted on total persons convicted gives a Pearsons coefficient of +508; Sig:

7   Ciccone, E., *The Trafficking flows and routes of Eastern Europe*, WEST Project (2005); R. Surtees, "Traffickers and Trafficking in Southern and Eastern Europe", *European Journal of Criminology*, vol. 5 (1): 39-68 (2008).

FIG. 12: **Correlation between the proportion of girls detected as victims and the proportion of women convicted for trafficking in persons,** during the period 2007-2010

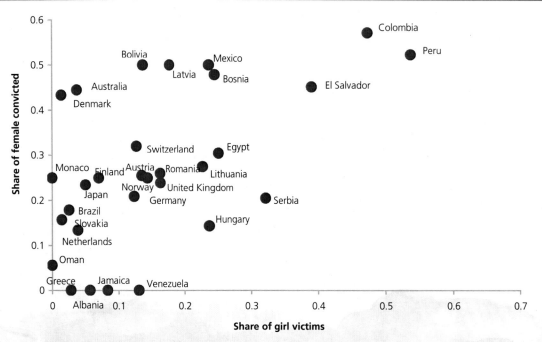

Source: UNODC elaboration of national data.

This has also been shown in other qualitative studies.[8] Trafficking networks also widely use women as recruiters of victims of sexual exploitation, as they may be more easily trusted by other females, who are more vulnerable to this type of trafficking.

This suggests that women traffickers are normally placed in low-ranking positions of the trafficking networks in order to carry out duties more exposed to the risk of being caught and prosecuted. As a consequence, a large share of women traffickers may also reflect the higher likelihood of this group being identified compared with male traffickers, as well as a possible investigative and prosecutorial focus on low-level perpetrators in some countries.[9]

●●

8   International Organization for Migration, Deceived Migrants from Tajikistan: A Study of Trafficking in Women and Children (Dushanbe, 2001); T. Denisova, ["Trafficking in Women and Children for Purposes of Sexual Exploitation"] United Nations Office on Drugs and Crime, *An Assessment of Referral Practices to Assist and Protect the Rights of Trafficked Persons in Moldova*; R. Surtees, "Traffickers and trafficking in Southern and Eastern Europe", *the European Journal of Criminology*, Volume 5 (1): 39-68 (2008); United Nations Interregional Crime and Justice Research Institute, *Trafficking in Women from Romania into Germany: Comprehensive Report*.

9   Organization for Security and Cooperation in Europe and the United Nations Global Initiative to Fight Human Trafficking, *Analysing the Business Model of Trafficking in Human Beings to Better Prevent the Crime (2010)*, pp. 56-58.

FIG. 13: **Activities where women were engaged in the trafficking process in Italy; share of the total number of females convicted between 1996 and 2003**

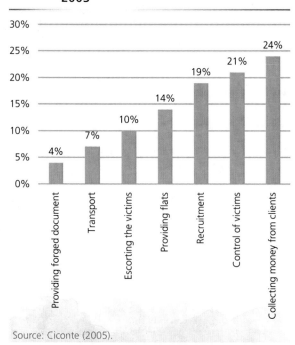

Source: Ciconte (2005).

For some women, previous voluntary involvement in prostitution may have led to their involvement in the operation of trafficking networks. This may not only have taught them the necessary skills about the trade but also provided exposure to the level of profits that may be derived from trafficking for sexual exploitation.[10] Other women may have themselves been trafficked and managed to "work their way up" to manage other victims.[11] The passage from the role of victim to the role of the exploiter has been documented, for instance, among Nigerian trafficking groups exploiting girls and women from Nigeria.[12] However, it is noted that victims who later become members of the criminal group exploiting other victims usually stay at the lower levels of the trafficking network's hierarchy. Such women may have another member of the same group still exploiting them.

Some countries do not report any differences concerning the gender profile of offenders in human trafficking as compared with other crimes. Moreover, qualitative studies have indicated that some trafficking networks have historically been male-driven, as in the case of Albanian trafficking groups.[13]

While women traffickers are more likely to be involved in the trafficking of girls for sexual exploitation, their prominence, as well as their roles in the trade, may change depending on a combination of factors. For example, the role of the country in the trafficking flow (e.g. country of origin of victims, destination country) may make female involvement more likely or less likely. Sociological factors, such as the broader roles of women in society, are also influential. The wide regional differences found in prosecutions and convictions reflect those different conditions.

Trafficking in persons in Eastern Europe and Central Asia, for example, has strong gender-specific characteristics, with the proportion of women among those prosecuted and convicted around and above 60 per cent throughout the whole reporting period, for all the countries considered. In other parts of the world, female offending rates

10 D. M. Hughes, and T. Denisova, *Trafficking in Women from Ukraine* (December 2003).

11 D. Siegel and S. de Blank, "Women who traffic women: the role of women in human trafficking networks – Dutch cases", *Global Crime*, 11:4, November 2010, 436-447.

12 J. Carling, *Migration, Human Smuggling and Trafficking from Nigeria to Europe* (International Organization for Migration, 2005); F. Carchedi, and I. Orfano, *La tratta di persone in Italia.* (Osservatorio Nazionale Tratta, 2007); United Nations Interregional Crime and Justice Research Institute, *Trafficking of Nigerian Girls to Italy* (2005).

13 E. Ciccone, *The Trafficking Flows and Routes of Eastern Europe* (WEST Project, 2005).

FIG. 14: **Proportion of men and women among those prosecuted and convicted of trafficking in persons, regional averages, 2007-2010**

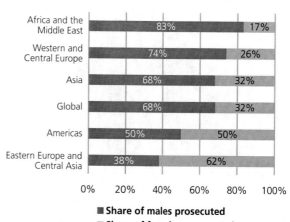

■ Share of males prosecuted
■ Share of females prosecuted

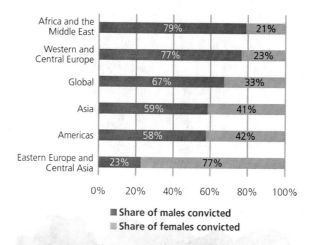

■ Share of males convicted
■ Share of females convicted

Source: UNODC elaboration of national data.

are much lower, for example in Western and Central Europe and in Africa and the Middle East.

Data on convictions and prosecutions show broadly similar patterns, even at regional/subregional levels, although women prosecuted in the Eastern Europe and Central Asia subregion are more likely to be convicted than men. Men in this subregion account for 38 per cent of the total number of prosecutions but only 23 per cent of convictions, whereas women account for 62 per cent of prosecutions and 77 per cent of convictions. Conversely, in the Americas, prosecuted women are less likely to be convicted. Women account for 50 per cent of prosecutions but only 42 per cent of convictions.

FIG. 15: **Proportion of own nationals and foreign nationals in persons convicted of trafficking in persons, selected countries, 2007-2010**

Citizenship of the traffickers, El Salvador

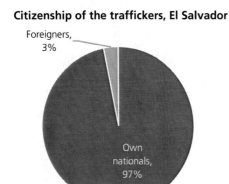

Source: Fiscalia General de la Republica-El Salvador

Citizenship of the traffickers, Japan

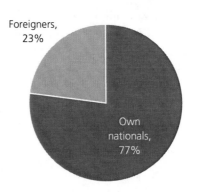

Source: Ministry of Justice -Japan.

Citizenship of the traffickers, Oman

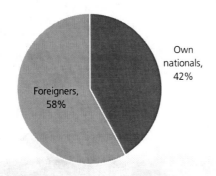

Source: National Committee for Combating Human Trafficking-Oman.

Citizenship of the traffickers, Denmark

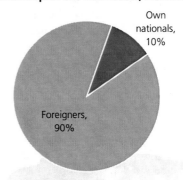

Source: Ministry of Justice-Denmark.

Less than 40 countries provided information on the nationalities of the persons convicted of human trafficking offences. Those data generally showed that own nationals comprised the vast majority of perpetrators. Foreign nationals constituted about one quarter of the total number of those convicted of trafficking in persons in all countries reporting. However, there are significant differences between countries. For example, while foreign nationals comprised 3 per cent of people convicted of trafficking in persons offences in El Salvador, in Oman, the proportion was 58 per cent.

There are also regional and subregional differences in the proportions of own nationals and foreign nationals among those convicted of trafficking in persons. For example, countries in Europe and the Middle East report larger proportions of foreign nationals among the detected

offenders. At the same time, countries within the same region may register significant differences in this respect, depending on the role of the country in the trafficking flow. Destination countries normally report a larger share of foreign nationals among those convicted. That is true for Gulf countries in the Middle East, Western European countries in general, Japan in East Asia and South Africa among the sub-Saharan countries.

However, differences in the proportion of own nationals versus foreign nationals among offenders cannot be explained only by the characteristics of the trafficking in the country considered. Countries record different levels of convictions of foreign nationals for all crimes — not only trafficking in persons. It is therefore necessary to compare the profile of offenders in trafficking in persons with those convicted of other crimes.

FIG. 16: **Shares of own nationals and foreign nationals in persons convicted of trafficking in persons, by country, selected countries, 2007-2010**

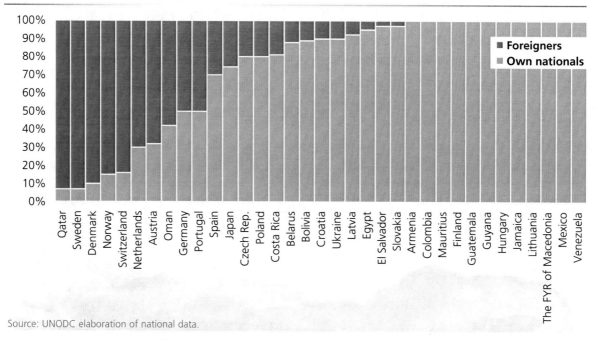

Source: UNODC elaboration of national data.

FIG. 17: **Shares of own nationals and foreign nationals in persons convicted of all crimes, selected countries, 2007-2010**

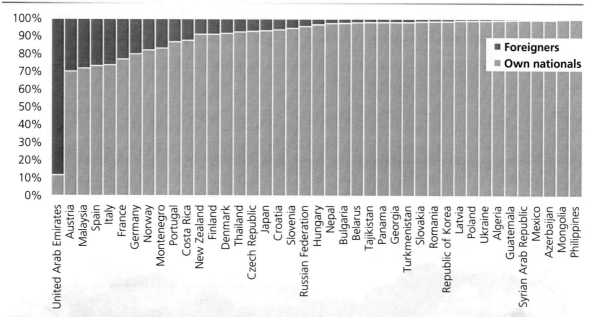

Source: UNODC, United Nations Survey of Crime Trends and Operations of Criminal Justice Systems.

In general, foreigners account for a limited share of convictions for all crimes. However, in Western Europe and some trafficking destination countries in the Middle East, the share of foreign nationals in total convictions is above the average. Those countries have large populations of foreign residents, which makes it statistically more probable that foreign nationals are more frequently convicted there than in other regions where the foreign population is lower.

The proportion of foreign offenders convicted of trafficking in persons is generally higher than for other crimes. While some 25 per cent of persons convicted of trafficking in persons were foreign nationals, the proportion of foreign nationals among people convicted for all crimes was about 10 per cent in the 41 countries responding to this question in the last United Nations Survey of Crime Trends and Operations of Criminal Justice Systems conducted by UNODC.

The proportion of foreign nationals convicted for all crimes is below 10 per cent in most regions, although the statistic for Europe is slightly higher. For human trafficking convictions, the percentage who are foreign nationals generally ranges between 5 and 20 per cent, but reaches 50-70 per cent in Western Europe, with peaks in Scandinavia, as well as in the Gulf countries of the Middle East.

The explanations for these differences in the nationality profiles of offenders may be similar to those identified for the gender profile. Just as it is a crime with strong gender connotations, trafficking in persons is also closely connected to migration. As presented below, foreign nationals account for more than three quarters of the total number of victims detected. That may help explain why foreign nationals, in some countries, are convicted more frequently for trafficking than for other crimes.

Nevertheless, it may also be that, in some countries, foreign nationals involved in trafficking are more likely to be detected than local traffickers. The mere fact of being foreign nationals may make foreign traffickers more visible and thus easier to detect.

To conclude, the profile of the offenders changes significantly from region to region and from country to country. In general, traffickers are more likely to be male and local nationals. However, the involvement of foreign nationals may be relatively prominent in destination countries. In terms of gender, women traffickers are more frequently implicated in the trafficking of girls.

3. Exploitation: the purpose of trafficking

As noted above, the definition of the crime of trafficking in persons contained in the Trafficking in Persons Protocol includes three elements: first, the act, which includes the recruitment, transportation, transfer, harbouring or receipt of persons; secondly, the means, including the threat or use of force or other forms of coercion, of abduction, of fraud, of deception, of the abuse of power or of a position of vulnerability or of the giving or receiving of payments or benefits to achieve the consent of a person having control over another person; and thirdly, the purpose, which is always exploitation, including, at a minimum, the exploitation of the prostitution of others or other forms of sexual exploitation, forced labour or services, slavery or practices similar to slavery, servitude and the removal of organs (Trafficking in Persons Protocol, article 3 (a)). From a criminological point of view, the exploitation is not only an element of the legal definition of the crime but also the motivation that drives the criminal to commit the crime.

Trafficking in persons happens mostly because of money as some human beings exploit others in order to gain profits. The traffickers leverage their power over the victims to force them to carry out certain tasks in conditions that the victims would not accept if they were free to decide. There are also some forms of human trafficking that are not economically motivated, such as trafficking for the removal of body parts for ritualistic purposes (see box on page 39).

Exploitation may take many forms. The Trafficking in Persons Protocol lists a number of purposes that the trafficking may have which, for the purpose of this report, have been grouped in three categories:

(a) Exploiting the prostitution of others or other forms of sexual exploitation;

(b) Forced labour or services, slavery or practices similar to slavery and servitude;

(c) Removal of organs.

Category **(a)** mainly includes the forms of exploitation aimed at obtaining economic profit from the forced commercial sexual activity of another person: the exploitation of the prostitution of others. It also includes cases that may be defined as sex slavery, although Member States have reported very few such cases.

With respect to category **(b)**, forced labour has been defined as "all work or service which is exacted from any person under the menace of any penalty and for which the said person has not offered himself voluntarily".[14] Slavery is defined in article 1 of the Slavery Convention of 1926,[15] as "the status or condition of a person over whom any or all of the powers attaching to the right of ownership are exercised". There is no internationally agreed definition of

14   Forced Labour Convention, 1930 (No. 29), of the International Labour Organization (United Nations, *Treaty Series, vol. 39, No. 612),* art. 2, para. 1.

15   United Nations, *Treaty Series, vol. 212, No. 2861.*

servitude, but the term is generally used to describe a condition of serfdom, without implying an element of ownership of the victim as the term "slavery" does.[16] These three different concepts are considered together in this report.

Category **(c)** refers to trafficking in persons aimed at the removal of human organs. The removal of human organs might be carried out for commercial purposes, such as the trade in organs for transplants.

The Trafficking in Persons Protocol indicated that the above-mentioned forms of exploitation should be considered, at a minimum, in national human trafficking legislation. By introducing the term "at a minimum" in the definition of the purposes of trafficking, Member States left open the option of including other or more specific purposes for which human trafficking was committed. In recent years, national legislation and jurisdictions have expanded the application of trafficking legislation. This has resulted in the inclusion of phenomena that existed long before the Protocol, such as child begging or the use of children to commit petty crimes, illegal adoptions[17] and forced marriages, among other things. Some countries reported cases of trafficking for the trading of body parts for rituals and/or traditional healing and medicine.

For the purpose of this report, these forms are grouped together under the term "other forms of trafficking". This category also includes mixed forms of exploitation, such as victims that were exploited for both forced labour and sexual exploitation.

Eighty-one countries reported information about the forms of exploitation of a total of 34,800 victims detected between 2007 and 2010 (or more recently, when available).

During the reporting period, countries in Europe and Central Asia and in the Americas reported detecting more victims of trafficking for sexual exploitation than for other forms of exploitation. Conversely, in Africa and the Middle

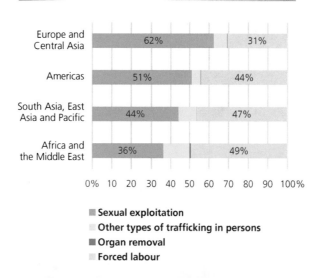

FIG. 18: **Forms of exploitation, proportion of the total number of detected victims, by region, 2007-2010**

- Sexual exploitation
- Other types of trafficking in persons
- Organ removal
- Forced labour

Source: UNODC elaboration of national data.

East and in South and East Asia and the Pacific, more victims of trafficking for forced labour were detected than for sexual exploitation.

The aggregated statistics for regions conceal the differences on the exploitative patterns in different individual countries. An analysis of these patterns at the national level shows that even within the same region or subregion, countries may register significant differences in the prevalence of the various forms of exploitation (see Map 4).

The share of victims trafficked for sexual exploitation globally during the reporting period ranged between 57 and 62 per cent of the total number of victims detected. The victims trafficked for forced labour accounted for about 31-36 per cent of the total. Victims trafficked for other purposes ranged between 5 and 8 per cent of the total victims detected in the period, while trafficking for organ removal accounted for about 0.1-0.2 per cent.

More countries reported information about the form of exploitation for 2010,[18] during which period about 58 per cent of the victims detected were trafficked for sexual exploitation. One victim in three was trafficked for forced

---

16 In Siliadin v France (2005), the European Court of Human Rights stated that servitude is a serious form of denial of freedom. It includes, in addition to the obligation to provide certain services to another, the obligation on the "serf" to live on the other's property and the impossibility of changing his status.

17 The interpretative notes on article 3 of the Trafficking in Persons Protocol (see A/55/383/Add.1, paras. 63-68) indicate that illegal adoption is to be considered as a purpose of trafficking where this amounts to a practice similar to slavery as defined in the Supplementary Convention on the Abolition of Slavery, the Slave Trade and Institutions and Practices Similar to Slavery (cited in *Travaux Préparatoires of the Negotiations for the Elaboration of the United Nations Convention against Transnational Organized Crime and the Protocols Thereto*, p. 347).

18 For 2010, 65 countries reported the form of exploitation of 9,000 detected victims. For other years, the data were as follows: for 2007, 31 countries and 6,600 victims; for 2008, 57 countries and 8,100 victims; for 2009, 58 countries and 9,200 victims; and for 2011, 13 countries and 1,800 victims.

MAP 4: **Main forms of exploitation, by proportion of detected victims, by country, 2007-2010**

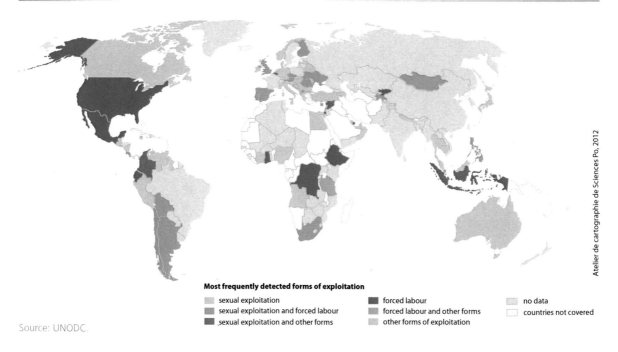

Most frequently detected forms of exploitation

sexual exploitation

sexual exploitation and forced labour

sexual exploitation and other forms

forced labour

forced labour and other forms

other forms of exploitation

no data

countries not covered

Atelier de cartographie de Sciences Po, 2012

Source: UNODC.

labour, slavery or servitude, while about 0.2 per cent of the victims detected were trafficked for the removal of organs. A relatively large share (6.4 per cent) of the victims detected in 2010 were trafficked for purposes not specifically mentioned in the Trafficking in Persons Protocol, such as begging, forced marriages, illegal adoption, participating in armed combat and committing crime (usually petty crime or street crime).

Global statistics on forms of exploitation show that trafficking in persons for purposes of sexual exploitation is more frequently detected than trafficking for forced labour. That result may not be fully representative of the real global situation, however, as countries in Europe and the Americas detect significantly more victims than do the other regions, with the result that exploitation patterns dominant in Europe and the Americas may be disproportionately reflected in global statistics. As a consequence, the proportion of trafficking for forced labour as calculated here (36 per cent) is likely to be underestimated, and trafficking for sexual exploitation is likely to be overestimated.

Furthermore, as indicated in the *Global Report on Trafficking in Persons* of 2009,[19] the lower rate of detection of

19 See UNODC/UN.GIFT, *Global Report on Trafficking in Persons (2009)*, p. 51.

FIG. 19: **Form of exploitation of all detected victims of trafficking in persons worldwide, 2010**

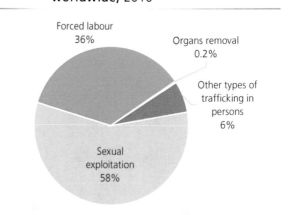

Forced labour
36%

Organs removal
0.2%

Other types of trafficking in persons
6%

Sexual exploitation
58%

Source: UNODC elaboration of national data.

trafficking in persons for forced labour as compared with sexual exploitation is probably due to the generally lower visibility of trafficking for forced labour, as well as historical limitations and/or partial nature of the legislation in many countries that until recently only considered trafficking for sexual exploitation.

However, the rate of detection of trafficking for forced labour is increasing. The *Global Report on Trafficking in Persons* of 2009 indicated that the proportion of detected victims who were trafficked for forced labour was about 18 per cent in 2006. That proportion appears to have doubled in the past few years, to 36 per cent of the total number of victims detected in 2010.

A clearly increasing trend can be noted in the short period 2007-2010, as the global share of detected victims exploited for the purpose of forced labour went from 31 to 36 per cent. Statistics for 2011 confirmed the increasing share of trafficking for forced labour compared with the previous years, keeping in mind, however, that this result was based on data from a limited sample of countries.

Given that many States introduced the offence of trafficking in persons for forced labour in their legislation after the entry into force of the Trafficking in Persons Protocol in 2003, that increase in the detection of trafficking for forced labour is not entirely surprising, as it is likely that authorities are now more aware of and have more experience in detecting such compared with the situation in 2006. Thus, the recorded increase in the share of trafficking for forced labour likely reflects an enhanced detection capacity rather than a real increase in the crime.

The proportion of victims trafficked for purposes other than forced labour and sexual exploitation doubled between 2006 and 2010, albeit that the proportion in 2006 was very low level. This increasing trend in trafficking for purposes not specifically listed in the Trafficking in Persons Protocol may indicate that national authorities are broadening the scope of their trafficking legislation. Within the category of trafficking for "other purposes", child begging is the form most frequently reported, accounting for about 1.5 cent of the total number of trafficking victims detected between 2007 and 2010. During that period, trafficking for begging was detected and reported in 19 countries around the world. Cases of trafficking for the purpose of illegal adoption have been detected in 15 countries. About 0.6 per cent of the total number of victims were trafficked for mixed sexual and labour exploitation. Trafficking in children for use as combatants appears to be concentrated in a limited number of countries. Cases of trafficking for forced marriages, for the production of pornographic material and for the use of body parts for rituals have also been reported in a number of countries.

Trafficking for the removal of organs may appear to be limited, as it accounts for less than 0.2 per cent of the total number of detected victims. Nonetheless, during the reporting period, cases or episodes of trafficking for organ

FIG. 20: **Form of exploitation of all victims detected for whom the form of exploitation was known, global, 2006 and 2010**

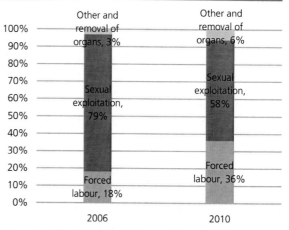

Source: UNODC/UN.GIFT and UNODC elaboration of national data.

Note: The results for 2006 are based on a sample of 10,568 detected victims whose form of exploitation was known: 8,320 were trafficked for sexual exploitation, 1,926 for forced labour, and 322 for organ removal and other forms of exploitation. The results for the 2010 are based on a sample of 9,007 detected victims whose form of exploitation was known: 5,189 were trafficked for sexual exploitation, 3,227 for forced labour and 591 for organ removal and other forms of exploitation.

FIG. 21: **Share of victims detected globally whose exploitation was known, by form of exploitation, 2007 to 2011**

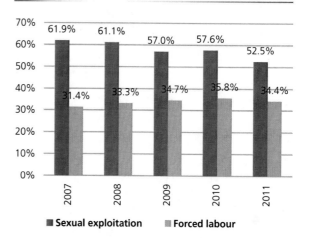

Source: UNODC elaboration of national data.

Note: The results are based on the following data. In 2007, of 6,600 victims detected, 4,084 were trafficked for sexual exploitation and 2,073 for forced labour. In 2008, of 8,100 victims detected, 4,993 were trafficked for sexual exploitation and 2,720 for forced labour. In 2009, of 9,200 victims detected, 5,229 were trafficked for sexual exploitation and 3,184 for forced labour. In 2010, of 9,007 victims detected, 5,189 were trafficked for sexual exploitation and 3,227 for forced labour. In 2011, of 1,800 victims detected, 1,015 were trafficked for sexual exploitation and 648 for forced labour.

MAP 5: Countries that report forms of exploitation other than sexual exploitation and forced labour, 2007-2010

■ Cases have been reported in the country   ▨ no data   ▨ countries not covered

Organ removal

Forced marriages

Body parts removal and rituals

Pornography

Begging and petty crimes

Child soldiers

Baby selling and illegal adoption

Mixed

Atelier de cartographie de Sciences Po, 2012

Source: UNODC.

Trafficking in organs and "muti" practices

Organ transplantations — particularly of kidneys but also of livers and hearts — are today commonplace in many countries, owing to their potential to prolong and improve lives. However, most countries face shortages of donor organs for use in such operations, and these shortages have given rise to an international organ trade. This trade has been found to follow established global patterns for commerce, with customers in more affluent countries obtaining organs from people in poorer countries. In fact, trafficking in organs had already been recognized as a significant health policy issue eight years ago, when Governments were urged to protect poor and vulnerable groups from the sale of organs.[a]

Organ trafficking is not classified as human trafficking. For an act to be considered trafficking in persons, a living person has to be recruited by means of force or deception for the exploitative purpose of removing an organ. There is a large grey area between licit organ donations and the trafficking of persons for organ removal. The removal and subsequent sale of organs from a corpse does not amount to human trafficking, as defined in the Trafficking in Persons Protocol, because the act of organ removal was not committed against a living person. It may not always be possible to ascertain the category to which organ removal and sale belong.

One particularly disturbing manifestation of organ-related crime is the mutilation of people to provide body parts for "*muti*" purposes. "*Muti*" is a broad term encompassing various forms of traditional "medicine" prepared and disbursed by healers without formal medical training. The belief that certain human body parts can improve health and/or prosperity is found particularly in parts of East and Southern Africa. In that context, body parts removed from a person who is alive are considered more potent than those from a corpse. Most people who are targeted for body parts are fatally injured, although a minority survive, often with severe injuries and health impairments.

As for trafficking in persons in general, women and children have been reported to be more frequently targeted for "*muti*" than men,[b] although these practices are conducted in secret, and there is very little official information available with which to establish victim profiles. People born with albinism may also be particularly vulnerable to "*muti*"-related crimes, especially in East Africa, as the body parts of albinos are considered by some to be particularly powerful, leaving the albino minority at a greater risk of exploitation.[c]

a   World Health Assembly resolution 57.18.
b   Chapter 10 ("Muti"), in International Organization for Migration, *No Experience Necessary: The Internal Trafficking of Persons in South Africa* (2008).
c   See, for example, Legal and Human Rights Centre, *Tanzania Human Rights Report 2009*.

removal were officially reported by 16 countries among those here considered. In addition, it appears that all regions are affected by trafficking for organ removal, which suggests that the phenomenon is not as marginal as the number of victims officially detected would suggest.

Core results: global baseline on trafficking patterns

- Adult women account for 55 to 60 per cent of all victims detected; females of every age for about 75 per cent.

- Child trafficking is frequently detected in Africa, and less frequently in Europe and the Americas. Children account for 27 per cent of all trafficking victims de-

tected globally. Out of every three child victims, two are girls and one is a boy.

- Adult men account for about 14 per cent of the detected victims of trafficking.

- In general, traffickers are adult males and local nationals of the country where the case is detected. Female traffickers and foreign traffickers are more prominent in trafficking in persons than in other crimes.

- Female traffickers are often involved in the trafficking of girls, and employed in low ranking activities that generally have a higher risk of detection.

- Trafficking for forced labour is the major detected form of trafficking in Africa and Asia. Sexual exploitation is more frequently detected in Europe and the Americas. Globally, trafficking for sexual exploitation accounts for 58 per cent of all trafficking cases detected, whereas trafficking for forced labour accounts for 36 per cent.

• The detection of trafficking for forced labour has been rapidly increasing over the last seven years.

• Victims trafficked for begging accounts for about 1.5 per cent of the victims detected globally, and trafficking for organ removal has been detected in 16 countries (among those here considered) in all regions of the world.

B. TRAFFICKING FLOWS: GLOBAL, LOCAL AND ACROSS ALL COUNTRIES

In this report, the term "trafficking flows" is used to discuss the geographical aspect of trafficking in persons. Given that this is a crime of global scope, it is highly relevant to analyse the origins and destinations of victims. Most countries that provided information for this report were able to identify the most common destination countries of their own nationals who were victims of trafficking, and the most common nationalities of trafficking victims detected in their countries. Governments also provided an indication of the level of domestic trafficking.

Analysis shows that this is a crime committed by people who abuse their power to exploit vulnerable persons for profit. Migrants may be discriminated, which often makes them vulnerable to trafficking. The data collected for this report show that about 73 per cent of victims of trafficking in persons detected around the world are exploited in a country not their own. Migrants and would-be-migrants tend to become vulnerable owing to their economic needs, their migratory status in terms of the legislation of the country in which they are exploited, language and cultural differences or the lack of a social network.

The analysis of the trafficking flows shows that, as a general pattern in recorded cases, victims are trafficked from poorer areas to richer areas. This is seen in a number of regions and subregions. For example, victims from poorer areas of Central America are trafficked to wealthier countries in Central America and North America. Victims are trafficked from the Andean countries to the countries of the Southern Cone, from the Balkan countries and Central Europe to Western Europe, from the poor countries in the Mekong river basin to wealthier countries in South-East Asia, and from South-East Asia to even wealthier

countries in Asia and the Pacific. The socioeconomic conditions of the victims and their hope of improving their lives abroad are among the factors of vulnerability that traffickers leverage to exploit them.

Communities of relative poverty exist in all countries, and there are people who may be potentially vulnerable to being trafficked, for different purposes, everywhere. Moreover, most forms of exploitation can take place in nearly any location. As a result, trafficking flows have the potential to affect all countries and regions worldwide.

The global dimension of trafficking in persons is difficult to assess because a trafficking flow may have any area of the world as its origin and any other as its destination. To compare, the flows related to other illicit markets, such as those of trafficking in opiates or cocaine, originate in a limited number of drug-producing countries. A similar situation exists with regard to firearms — for which there are a limited number of manufacturing countries — and with regard to some types of environmental crime restricted to areas where certain natural resources abound. While most other types of trafficking have geographical limitations with respect to sources or destination markets, trafficking in persons does not.

That lack of geographical boundaries is reflected in the large number of countries affected by trafficking in persons, usually by means of multiple trafficking flows. A "trafficking flow" is defined as a link, established on the basis of documented episodes of trafficking in persons, connecting the origin of the detected victims with the victims' destination. Approximately 460 distinct trafficking flows[20] can be identified in the period 2007-2010 (or more recently). During that period, victims of 136 different nationalities were detected in 118 countries across the world.

This information represents only the part of the trafficking activity that is recorded in the official records of the Member States that shared their data with UNODC. Taking that into account, it is clear that the complexity of trafficking flows reported in this report represents the real situation only partially and that there are many human trafficking flows not captured in the data presented.

• •

20 For the purpose of this report, a "trafficking flow" is defined as the line connecting two locations: the origin and the destination of at least five victims of trafficking in cases documented during the reporting period. A trafficking flow is also considered to exist when national authorities reported that destination or that origin as commonly documented during the reporting period, even if no specific numbers were provided. Trafficking flows thus defined also include two locations within the same country. If the threshold for a trafficking flow were set at one detected victim, the number of trafficking flows emerging from the data collected would be about 870 between 2007 and 2010.

Trafficking in persons is a global, transnational phenomenon with different national and international manifestations. It emerges from local situations, often evolving into cross-border trafficking between neighbouring countries or countries within the same region and sometimes leads to long-distance transcontinental flows. The characteristics of the crime are constantly changing, creating a complex and evolving web of trafficking flows worldwide.

It is not possible to categorize countries exclusively as areas of origin or destination of trafficking in persons. With a few exceptions, most countries are both origins of human trafficking towards other destinations as well as destinations for people trafficked from other countries simultaneously. Additionally, many countries also have significant levels of domestic trafficking, where the international dimension is not relevant.

The following sections will present an analysis of trafficking flows as they emerge from the data that underpin this report. Section I.B.1 describes the flows from the vantage point of destinations. For each country or region, the origin of the victims detected in the country or region is presented. Section I.B.2 analyses the situation from the perspective of the origin. For each major nationality (or regional/subregional group), the destination of the trafficked victims of that nationality is discussed. The case of domestic trafficking is analysed in a third section.

1. Trafficking flows at the destination: where do the victims come from?

For the preparation of the present report, 83 countries provided information on the nationality of 26,700 victims detected in their territory between 2007 and 2010 (or more recently). A total of 136 different nationalities of victims were identified.

About 27 per cent of all detected victims were trafficked within the country where they were exploited. According to the regional aggregation used for this report, 45 per cent of the victims detected during the same period were trafficked from other countries within the same subregion. Four per cent of the total number of victims detected originated in a nearby subregion (for instance, South Americans trafficked to North America, or sub-Saharan Africans trafficked to the Middle East), thus about half of the trafficking victims globally are trafficked within the same region.[21] About a quarter of the detected victims that

21   Regional aggregations necessarily bring some level of approximation.

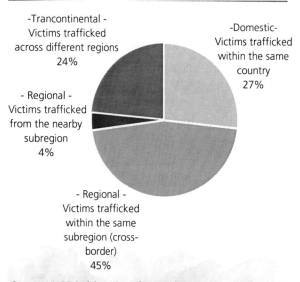

FIG. 22: **Domestic, regional and transregional flows of trafficking in persons**, 2007-2010 (percentage of all trafficking flows)

-Trancontinental - Victims trafficked across different regions 24%

-Domestic- Victims trafficked within the same country 27%

- Regional - Victims trafficked from the nearby subregion 4%

- Regional - Victims trafficked within the same subregion (cross-border) 45%

Source: UNODC elaboration of national data.

originated in one region were exploited in other regions (for instance, Asians in the Americas or Europeans in Asia).

Geographical proximity clearly influences human trafficking flows, as more than 75 per cent of the trafficking flows considered in this report can be defined as being of short or medium range. The data show that victims tend to be trafficked within the same region — domestically or across a border — much more frequently than to other regions.

This may be explained largely in terms of convenience and risk minimization for the trafficker. As discussed above, migrants are generally more vulnerable to exploitation than local citizens. At the same time, exploiting foreign nationals from a nearby country reduces the costs and risks associated with the transportation of the person to be exploited. Long-distance trafficking flows need to be supported by a well-structured organization that can take care of air travel and false documents and that sometimes also exercises long-distance control over the families of the victims in the origin country. This form of trafficking cannot be sustained over time unless a structured trafficking network is in place. Exploiting a foreign national from a nearby country appears to be much easier than exploiting a local resident or a person trafficked from another continent.

••

Countries that are geographically close may be categorized into different regions, while others may be distant but still placed in the same region. The countries list and their regional aggregation are reported in table contained in the introduction of this report.

MAP 6: **Shares of detected victims who were trafficked within or from outside the region,** 2007-2010

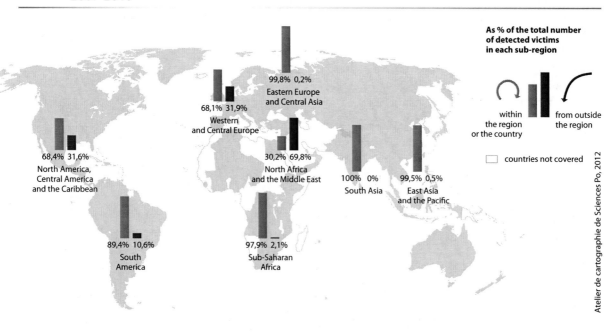

Source: UNODC.

MAP 7: **Countries of origin of victims detected in Western and Central Europe,** 2007-2010

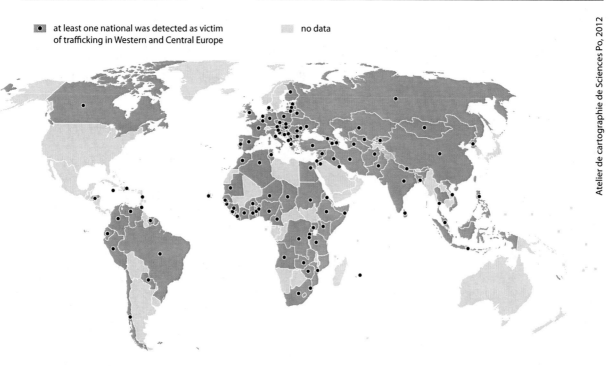

Source: UNODC.

Atelier de cartographie de Sciences Po, 2012

Atelier de cartographie de Sciences Po, 2012

Trafficking in persons is a global, transnational phenomenon with different national and international manifestations. It emerges from local situations, often evolving into cross-border trafficking between neighbouring countries or countries within the same region and sometimes leads to long-distance transcontinental flows. The characteristics of the crime are constantly changing, creating a complex and evolving web of trafficking flows worldwide.

It is not possible to categorize countries exclusively as areas of origin or destination of trafficking in persons. With a few exceptions, most countries are both origins of human trafficking towards other destinations as well as destinations for people trafficked from other countries simultaneously. Additionally, many countries also have significant levels of domestic trafficking, where the international dimension is not relevant.

The following sections will present an analysis of trafficking flows as they emerge from the data that underpin this report. Section I.B.1 describes the flows from the vantage point of destinations. For each country or region, the origin of the victims detected in the country or region is presented. Section I.B.2 analyses the situation from the perspective of the origin. For each major nationality (or regional/subregional group), the destination of the trafficked victims of that nationality is discussed. The case of domestic trafficking is analysed in a third section.

1. Trafficking flows at the destination: where do the victims come from?

For the preparation of the present report, 83 countries provided information on the nationality of 26,700 victims detected in their territory between 2007 and 2010 (or more recently). A total of 136 different nationalities of victims were identified.

About 27 per cent of all detected victims were trafficked within the country where they were exploited. According to the regional aggregation used for this report, 45 per cent of the victims detected during the same period were trafficked from other countries within the same subregion. Four per cent of the total number of victims detected originated in a nearby subregion (for instance, South Americans trafficked to North America, or sub-Saharan Africans trafficked to the Middle East), thus about half of the trafficking victims globally are trafficked within the same region.[21] About a quarter of the detected victims that

••

21 Regional aggregations necessarily bring some level of approximation.

FIG. 22: **Domestic, regional and transregional flows of trafficking in persons**, 2007-2010 (percentage of all trafficking flows)

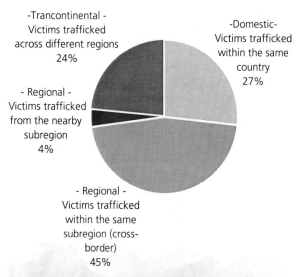

-Trancontinental - Victims trafficked across different regions 24%

-Domestic- Victims trafficked within the same country 27%

- Regional - Victims trafficked from the nearby subregion 4%

- Regional - Victims trafficked within the same subregion (cross-border) 45%

Source: UNODC elaboration of national data.

originated in one region were exploited in other regions (for instance, Asians in the Americas or Europeans in Asia).

Geographical proximity clearly influences human trafficking flows, as more than 75 per cent of the trafficking flows considered in this report can be defined as being of short or medium range. The data show that victims tend to be trafficked within the same region — domestically or across a border — much more frequently than to other regions.

This may be explained largely in terms of convenience and risk minimization for the trafficker. As discussed above, migrants are generally more vulnerable to exploitation than local citizens. At the same time, exploiting foreign nationals from a nearby country reduces the costs and risks associated with the transportation of the person to be exploited. Long-distance trafficking flows need to be supported by a well-structured organization that can take care of air travel and false documents and that sometimes also exercises long-distance control over the families of the victims in the origin country. This form of trafficking cannot be sustained over time unless a structured trafficking network is in place. Exploiting a foreign national from a nearby country appears to be much easier than exploiting a local resident or a person trafficked from another continent.

••

Countries that are geographically close may be categorized into different regions, while others may be distant but still placed in the same region. The countries list and their regional aggregation are reported in table contained in the introduction of this report.

MAP 6:   Shares of detected victims who were trafficked within or from outside the region, 2007-2010

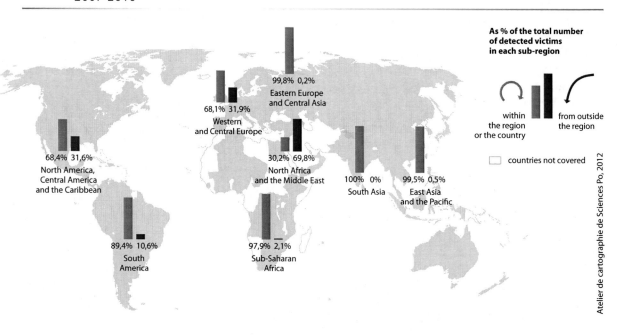

As % of the total number of detected victims in each sub-region

within the region or the country

from outside the region

countries not covered

Atelier de cartographie de Sciences Po, 2012

North America, Central America and the Caribbean — 68,4% 31,6%

South America — 89,4% 10,6%

Western and Central Europe — 68,1% 31,9%

Eastern Europe and Central Asia — 99,8% 0,2%

North Africa and the Middle East — 30,2% 69,8%

Sub-Saharan Africa — 97,9% 2,1%

South Asia — 100% 0%

East Asia and the Pacific — 99,5% 0,5%

Source: UNODC.

MAP 7:   Countries of origin of victims detected in Western and Central Europe, 2007-2010

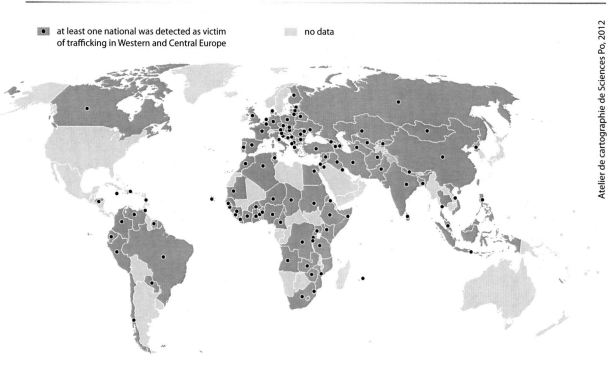

at least one national was detected as victim of trafficking in Western and Central Europe

no data

Atelier de cartographie de Sciences Po, 2012

Source: UNODC.

MAP 8: **Share of detected victims trafficked from other regions, 2007-2010**

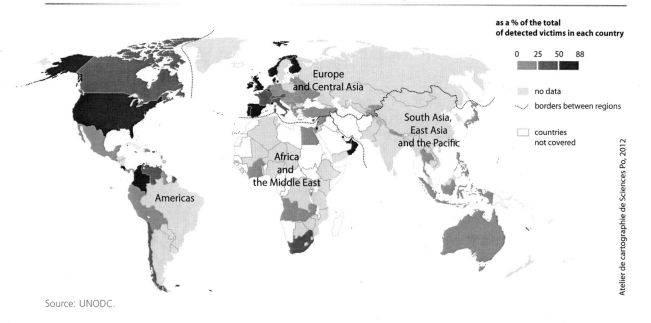

Source: UNODC.

The region of Europe and Central Asia, as used in the present analysis — is divided into two subregions: Western and Central Europe, and Eastern Europe and Central Asia. Those two subregions have different profiles of incoming human trafficking flows. Almost all the victims trafficked to countries of Eastern Europe and Central Asia are nationals of that subregion, either trafficked domestically or from other countries within the subregion. According to the data collected for this report, domestic trafficking accounted for a significant part of the victims detected in this subregion.

About 70 per cent of the victims detected in Western and Central Europe are European, and the 64 per cent of them are trafficked from countries of Western and Central European countries. Owing to the limited geographical size of this subregion, it is clear that the bulk of the victims detected there are trafficked from countries close to the destination. Domestic trafficking in Western and Central Europe appears to be less prominent than in the other regions. Nonetheless, one of four victims detected in the subregion between 2007 and 2010 was a national of the country where he or she was exploited.

Western and Central Europe displays the widest variety of origins or distance of the trafficking flows. During the reporting period, in the subregion victims of 112 different nationalities were detected, including more than 70 non-European nationalities (see Map 7).

Countries in the Americas reported that in the period considered a large part of the incoming trafficking was of domestic origin or of victims from other countries in the region. More than 75 per cent of the victims detected in the region are nationals of a country in the region. Moreover, most of the trafficking takes place within the two subregions that comprise the region. About 88 per cent of the victims detected in South America are South Americans, while 65 per cent of the victims detected in countries in North and Central America and the Caribbean are North Americans, Central Americans or nationals of the Caribbean. In each subregion, there are countries that are more predominantly reported to be origin countries, as well as other countries more frequently mentioned as destinations, although most of the trafficking occurs among neighbouring countries.

The Americas is also a receiver of victims of transcontinental trafficking, in particular North America, where one third of the detected victims are from outside the region. Between 2007 and 2010, victims of 44 different nationalities were detected by countries of the Western Hemisphere, including victims of 20 nationalities outside the region. Asian victims, for example, have been detected in different countries in the Americas and are prominent in the United States of America. In particular, East Asian victims accounted for 22 per cent of the detected victims in the Americas.

Do economic dynamics affect trafficking in persons?

In the preamble to the United Nations Global Plan of Action against Trafficking in Persons, the General Assembly recognizes that "poverty, unemployment, lack of socioeconomic opportunities, gender-based violence, discrimination and marginalization are some of the contributing factors that make persons vulnerable to trafficking in persons". (Assembly resolution 64/293).

Poverty and unemployment are considered to be among the factors of vulnerability linked to trafficking in persons, factors that are alluded to throughout this report. A commonly observed human trafficking pattern is that victims are often trafficked from relatively poorer to comparatively richer areas. Far fewer victims are trafficked in the opposite direction. Not all trafficking flows fit this pattern, however, and economic differences alone cannot explain the whole trafficking phenomenon. Nonetheless, economic differences in combination with geographical proximity appear to explain many of the trafficking flows identified and discussed in this report.

Along this line of analysis, one pertinent question is whether economic dynamics can explain increases or reductions of certain trafficking flows. Can changes — positive or negative — in the socioeconomic conditions in a particular country explain, at least partially, the shifts in human trafficking flows originating in that country?

The hypothesis is that an improvement in the economic and labour opportunities in origin countries reduces the number of persons willing to risk unsafe working opportunities. Assuming that all other factors remained equal, this would reduce the number of victims from such countries of origin that are detected at destination. Vice versa, in times of economic crisis, more people would be expected to take such risks, meaning that more victims from those countries would be detected at destination.

It is difficult to confirm or reject this hypothesis, first of all because of the lack of reliable data. Secondly, it is difficult to isolate economic dynamics from the myriad other variables that may potentially affect trafficking flows.

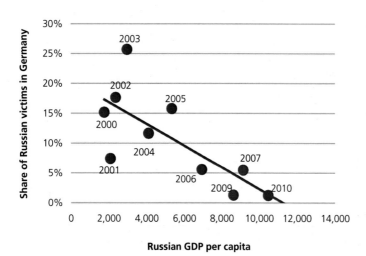

Linear Regression:
Share of Russian victims in Germany= 0.205 - 1.84E-05* Russian GDP per capita; R - Square = 0.55

For subregions and countries where relevant and reliable time series data are available, it is possible to discern some human trafficking flows that seem to respond to socioeconomic changes. For instance, Eastern European victims are nowadays less frequently detected in Western and Central Europe than over the past decade. This may be at least partially due to the improved economic conditions in Eastern Europe compared with the late 1990s. There is, for example, a positive statistical correlation between the unemployment rates of the Russian Federation and Ukraine and the share of Russian and Ukrainian victims detected in the Netherlands.[a] In addition, Germany recorded a decreasing trend in the share of Russian victims detected, while simultaneously, Russian per capita GDP increased.[b]

The same result is found between the share of Lithuanian victims detected in Germany and the Lithuanian per capita GDP.[c] Similarly, there is also a correlation between the reduction in the number of Thai victims detected in Germany[d] and Indonesian victims in Japan[e] and the lower unemployment rates in Thailand and Indonesia, respectively.

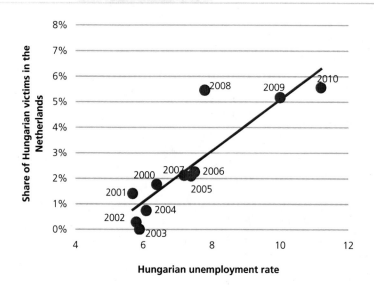

Hungarian unemployment rate

Linear Regression:
Share of Hungarian victims = -6.65E-02 + 1.261E-02 * Hungarian
unemployment rate; R - Square= 0.861

Were such a relation to exist, it should be observable also in times of economic crisis. Hungary is not a major origin of trafficking. Hungarian victims have rarely been detected outside Western and Central Europe, where they account for just about 3 per cent of the total detected victims. This share has been increasing in recent years, however. In the Netherlands, for example, the share of Hungarian victims among the total number of detected victims increased from less than 1.5 per cent to 5 per cent. At the same time, the Hungarian unemployment rate increased, from 5.5 per cent in 2001 to 11 per cent in 2010. A closer look at the statistics suggests that the dynamics of these two phenomena are linked.[f] A similar analysis regarding the number of Bulgarian victims detected in the Netherlands[g] confirms this pattern, including during the recent years of economic downturn in Bulgaria.

While these correlations are noteworthy, they are not sufficient for defining a general pattern. Even if further analyses were to confirm the hypothesis put forward here, economic dynamics alone cannot fully explain the evolution of the complex crime of human trafficking and its multiple manifestations worldwide. Economic data should, however, be used to provide a fundamental analytical context in order to assess the adoption or absence of policies and their impact. Collecting more and better data would thus not only foster a greater understanding of the dynamics of trafficking in persons but also enhance international efforts to prevent it through solid, evidence-based policies.

a   There is a significant and positive correlation between the percentage of Ukrainian victims detected in the Netherlands (Dutch National Rapporteur, 2000-2010) and Ukrainian unemployment rates (World Bank) for the period 2000-2010 (Pearson's coefficient equal to 0.649, and Sig. 2-tailed: 0.042). Similar results are obtained for the share of Russian victims detected in the Netherlands and Russian unemployment rates during the same period (Pearson: 0.646, Sig.: 0.044). Univariate regression analyses confirm a partial link between these variables.

b   There is a significant and negative correlation between the percentage of Russian victims detected in Germany (Bundeslagebild Menschenhandel, 2000-2010) and Russian per capita gross domestic product for the period 2000-2010 (Pearson: -0.674, Sig.: 0.047). Univariate regression analysis is significant and confirms the partial link.

c   There is a significant and negative correlation between the percentage of Lithuanian victims detected in Germany (Bundeslagebild Menschenhandel, 2000-2010) and Lithuania per capita gross domestic product for the period 2000-2010 (Pearson: -0.793, Sig.: 0.034). Univariate regression analysis is significant and confirms the partial link.

d   There is a significant and positive correlation between the percentage of Thai victims detected in Germany and Thai unemployment rates for the period 2000-2010 (Pearson: 0.929; Sig.: 0.001). Univariate regression analysis is significant and confirms the partial link.

e   There is a significant and positive correlation between the percentage of Indonesian victims detected in Japan (National Police data, 2000-2010) and Indonesian unemployment rates for the period 2000 to 2010 (Pearson: 0.694; Sig.: 0.026). A regression analysis is significant and confirms the partial link.

f   There is a significant and positive correlation between the percentage of Hungarian victims detected in the Netherlands and Hungarian unemployment rates for the period 2000-2010 (Pearson: 0.879; Sig.: 0.000). Univariate regression analyses are significant and confirm the partial link.

g   There is a significant and positive correlation between the percentage of Bulgarian victims detected in the Netherlands and Bulgarian unemployment rates for the period 2000-2010 (Pearson: 0.659; Sig.: 0.027). Univariate regression analyses are significant and confirm the partial link.

Between 2007 and 2010, countries of South and East Asia and the Pacific predominantly detected Asian victims. More than 99 per cent of the victims detected in South and East Asia were trafficked either domestically or within South Asia and East Asia, respectively. This is also true for the rich destination countries of Asia and the Pacific, where victims from other regions were very rarely detected during the reporting period. Compared with the overall number of victims detected in Asian countries, non-Asian victims were relatively few.

A large part of the trafficking reported in sub-Saharan Africa between 2007 and 2010 was intraregional. The subregion recorded a large share of domestic trafficking, where such trafficking accounted for about 40 per cent of the total number of detected victims. Conversely, interregional trafficking is very prominent in the Middle East subregion. Based on the data collected for this report, about 70 per cent of the victims detected in the subregion are nationals from other regions. Between 2007 and 2010, in the Middle East, victims from about 40 different nationalities were detected, including about 20 countries outside Africa and the Middle East (mainly Asians and Europeans).

Although globally, most victims originate in countries within the same region, long-distance trafficking flows should not be ignored. Trafficking in persons originating in regions other than the destination region account for about 24 per cent of all victims detected globally.

Map 8 shows that certain areas of the world have a higher prevalence of trafficking victims from other regions. Such trafficking accounts for the majority of the victims detected in more than 12 of the 83 countries that reported the nationality of the victims. More than 20 countries reported a prevalence of long-distance trafficking above the world average of 24 per cent.

2. Trafficking flows at the origin:
where are victims trafficked to?

In order to analyse the characteristics of the trafficking flows from the perspective of the origin countries, two types of data are considered. One is the nationality of the victims detected in the countries of destination: the same information provided by 83 countries on the citizenship of the nearly 27,000 victims detected between 2007 and 2010 that was used in the preceding analysis. The other regards the countries from which repatriated trafficked victims were returned. In this category, 31 countries reported on own nationals who had been identified as

victims of trafficking in other countries and repatriated between 2007 and 2010. Those countries reported about 9,300 victims who had been repatriated from about 90 different destination countries.[22]

The global nature of trafficking in persons becomes apparent through this type of analysis. Combining the two information sources mentioned above shows that victims of 136 different nationalities were detected in 118 countries worldwide, as previously indicated. Moreover, about 460 different trafficking flows were detected globally between 2007 and 2010.

These trafficking flows are all unique, although some broad similarities can be noted, particularly at the subregional level. Some areas experience mainly "outbound" trafficking, with large number of victims trafficked to other regions, whereas others report mainly intraregional trafficking. Moreover, some areas of origin see a relatively large number of victims trafficked to one particular or a few destinations, even if the destinations where these victims were trafficked vary depending on the nationalities and regions of origin.

The data regarding the place of detection or repatriation of certain nationalities of victims support the analysis in the previous section. According to the data collected for this report, human trafficking is largely comprised of foreign nationals trafficked to neighbouring countries or countries within their regions of origin. Certain nationalities were significantly detected in regions other than their own, however. This is the case for East and South Asians, sub-Saharan Africans and South Americans.

Figure 23 represents the geographical diffusion of the trafficking flows according to nationality of the victims. The key value considered is the number of countries detecting the nationalities of the region during the period considered, regardless of how many victims were detected. The figure distinguishes between destinations within the region and outside the region, and this last indicator displays the diffusion of the trafficking flows globally.

This figure is based on information obtained by combining the data on the victims of trafficking reported in the countries of destination and the data on repatriated victims.

22 The two sources are treated separately and combined appropriately when the analysis allows. To avoid double-counting, the combination of the two sources is used to display — not measure — the number of nationalities of victims and the number of countries of destination where the victims were either detected or repatriated from.

FIG. 23: **Diffusion of the trafficking flows within and out of the region of origin** (n: number of countries where these nationals were detected or repatriated from); 2007-2010

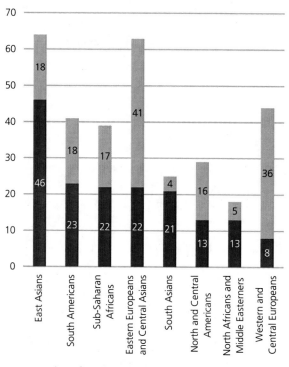

- ■ **Number of countries within the region detecting these nationals**
- ■ **Number of countries outside the region detecting these nationals**

Source: UNODC elaboration of national data.

Nationals from Western and Central Europe are almost exclusively detected in Europe, with a limited number of countries detecting these nationals outside their region. Victims from North and Central America and the Caribbean were detected in 13 countries outside their region, as were victims from North Africa or the Middle East.

East and South Asians, South Americans, sub-Saharan Africans and Eastern Europeans have been widely detected at the international level outside their own regions of origin. It can be concluded that these are the more widely trafficked nationalities at the global level.

The above observation reinforces the argument that socio-economic factors are important to consider when trying to understand vulnerability in relation to trafficking in persons. Victims from less developed areas tend to be traf-

ficked to more affluent countries or regions. Transregional trafficking affects victims from poor countries, with rich countries more frequently being the destination. Victims from the poorer parts of Europe or North America are often trafficked intraregionally (i.e. within the region), and rarely to the "global South".

The diffusion of the human trafficking flows — in other words, how various flows spread from a given source — is just one indicator of the dimension of the flows at the international level. Another element to take into account is the severity of the flow. As map 9 shows, not all the nationalities indicated above as being those of victims trafficked to a wide range of international destinations are detected in the same volume. While some victims of some nationalities account for a significant proportion of trafficking victims in some destination countries, victims of other nationalities are detected in small numbers in a variety of countries.

Combining the data on the diffusion of the trafficking flows (figure 23) with the data on the severity of the flow at destination (map 9) is useful to analyse the specific geographical characteristics of the flows originating from the different areas of the world, and to assess their relevance at the global level.

An analysis of the diffusion of the human trafficking flows originating from sub-Saharan Africa reveals that the trafficking of African victims has countries of Africa, the Middle East and Europe as its main destinations. While 19 European countries detected African victims between 2007 and 2010, few countries in other regions did so. Victims from sub-Saharan Africa account for a large share of the victims detected in Western and Central Europe (15 per cent) and in the Middle East (20 per cent), but less than 1 per cent of the victims detected in the other regions. Thus, it seems that human trafficking originating in Africa has not developed into a global phenomenon: in geographical terms, it is strongly linked but limited to Africa, the Middle East and Western Europe.

Conversely, the trafficking flows originating in Eastern Europe and Central Asia appear to be relatively dispersed inside and outside the European continent. Nationals from the subregion were widely trafficked in Western and Central Europe, and they were detected or repatriated from 13 countries in Africa and the Middle East, six countries in the Americas and three countries in East Asia and the Pacific. When this information is combined with data on the number of victims detected at destinations, however,

MAP 9:   Transnational flows: Nationalities of victims detected in some major destination regions, shares of the total number of victims detected there, 2007-20100

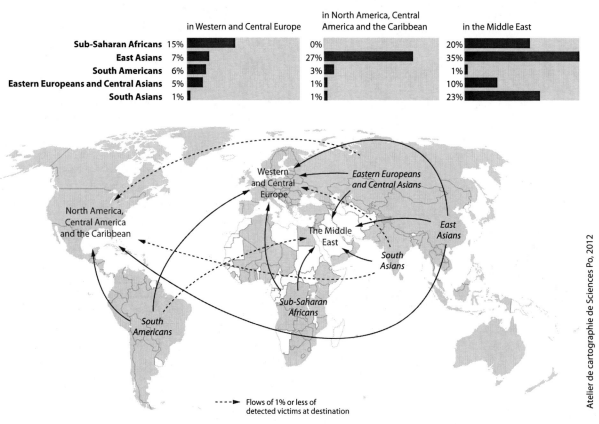

	in Western and Central Europe	in North America, Central America and the Caribbean	in the Middle East
Sub-Saharan Africans	15%	0%	20%
East Asians	7%	27%	35%
South Americans	6%	3%	1%
Eastern Europeans and Central Asians	5%	1%	10%
South Asians	1%	1%	23%

- - - ▶ Flows of 1% or less of
detected victims at destination

Source: UNODC.

Atelier de cartographie de Sciences Po, 2012

the severity of the phenomenon seems to be limited compared with other flows. Eastern Europeans and Central Asians account for about 5 per cent of the victims detected in Western and Central Europe, 10 per cent in the Middle East and less than 1 per cent in the Americas and Asia.

Victims from South America were mainly detected in or repatriated from countries in the region, which confirms the largely intraregional character of trafficking in that subregion. In terms of long-distance trafficking, trafficking flows of South American origin appear to be quite widely spread around the world. During the reporting period, South American victims were detected in 16 countries in Europe, as well as in six countries in Asia and in one country in the Middle East. In terms of severity, South American victims account for 6 per cent of the victims detected in Western and Central Europe, 3 per cent of victims in North and Central America and the Caribbean and much less than 1 per cent in the other regions. Victims from Central America and the Caribbean were also

detected in Europe and in three countries in the Middle East, although in relatively low numbers.

South Asian victims were trafficked to at least 14 European countries, five countries in Africa and the Middle East and two in the Americas. In terms of severity of the trafficking flows outside their region of origin, a significant number of South Asians are trafficked to the Middle East, where they account for more than 20 per cent of the all victims detected.

The data collected for this report also show that trafficking in persons originating in East Asia is the most widely diffused flow globally. During the reporting period, East Asian victims were detected in or repatriated from at least 64 countries worldwide, including 46 countries outside the Asia-Pacific region. East Asian victims have been detected or repatriated from 18 countries in Europe and Central Asia, 13 countries in the Americas and 14 countries in Africa and the Middle East.

MAP 10: **Countries where East Asian victims were detected, 2007-2010**

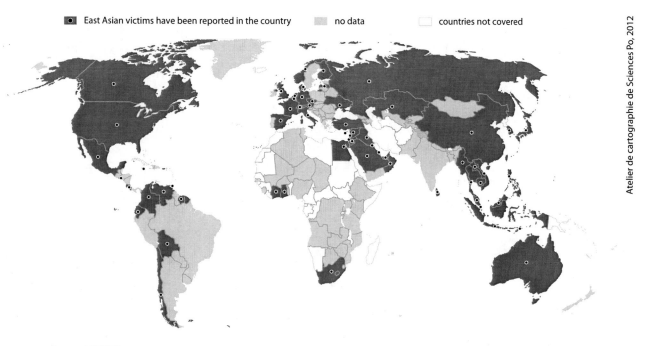

■● East Asian victims have been reported in the country   no data   countries not covered

Atelier de cartographie de Sciences Po, 2012

Source: UNODC.

Trafficked victims from East Asia are not only widely detected in terms of geographical destination but they are also detected in relatively large numbers worldwide. East Asians account for about 7 per cent of the detected victims in Western and Central Europe, 27 per cent of the detected trafficking in North and Central America, and 35 per cent of the trafficking in the Middle East. Moreover, East Asians accounted for about 10 per cent of the victims detected in South America, and for more than 1 per cent of the victims detected in sub-Saharan Africa.

The global dimension of East Asian trafficking, in particular, was already documented in the *Global Report on Trafficking in Persons* of 2009.[23] Between 2007 and 2010, East Asian nationals were detected in many destination countries, in all regions and subregions considered in this report, including parts of the world that are not normally considered destinations of transcontinental trafficking, such as sub-Saharan Africa. Map 10 shows the countries where East Asian trafficking victims were reported, detected or repatriated from during the reporting period.

The significance of the trafficking flows originating in East Asia is further confirmed when the number of victims

detected globally is taken into consideration. More than 5,000 East Asian victims were detected between 2007 and 2010 by the authorities of the 83 destination countries that reported on the nationality of detected victims. East Asian victims comprise 20 per cent of all the victims reported for the purpose of the present report. This result is noteworthy, considering that just six countries[24] from the populous East Asia and the Pacific subregion reported the nationality of the victims detected. Assuming that East Asian countries are largely detecting East Asians victims, this would mean that a significant number of detected East Asian victims are still missing from the data upon which this report is based. It also suggests that the trafficking of East Asian victims remains, in terms of diffusion as well as severity, the most prominent human trafficking flow at the global level.

3. The case of domestic trafficking

While most of the victims detected around the world were foreign nationals in their country of exploitation, about

- -
23 UNODC/UN.GIFT (2009).

- -
24 The six countries of East Asia and the Pacific that, for the purpose of this report, provided information on the nationality of the victims detected were Australia, Indonesia, Japan, the Philippines, Singapore and Thailand.

one in every four victims detected between 2007 and 2010 was a national of the country where he or she was exploited. The presence and relevance of domestic trafficking in certain countries challenges one common understanding of this phenomenon. Although the term "trafficking in persons" may suggest that the victim is moved to a different location, by definition, this does not necessarily need to happen. According to the definition of trafficking in persons in the Trafficking in Persons Protocol,[25] the victim may be "recruited" or "harboured" for the purpose of exploitation by means of coercion or other means that do not necessarily include movement. Furthermore, even when the definition of trafficking addresses the movement of the victim ("transfer", "transport" and "receipt") there is no specification that this movement has to be across borders.

The data show that domestic trafficking is relatively prominent. During the reporting period, victims trafficked within the country of origin accounted for more than 25 per cent of the total number of all detected victims. Furthermore, when the geographical diffusion of internal trafficking is considered, it can be seen that it is a global phenomenon. Such trafficking has been reported in more than 60 of the 83 countries worldwide reporting information on the nationality of the victims.

Moreover, domestic trafficking appears to be increasing. In the light of the information collected during the reporting period, considered by year, the share of domestic trafficking detected increased.[26]

The increasing trend in the number of own nationals detected as trafficking victims, as well as the increasing number of countries detecting domestic trafficking, may be caused by a combination of factors. One such factor might be that cross-border trafficking is becoming increasingly difficult as a result of more efficient controls at the borders. It is also possible that traffickers may find it more difficult to recruit from traditional origin countries as

MAP 11: **Countries where domestic trafficking was detected, 2007-2010**

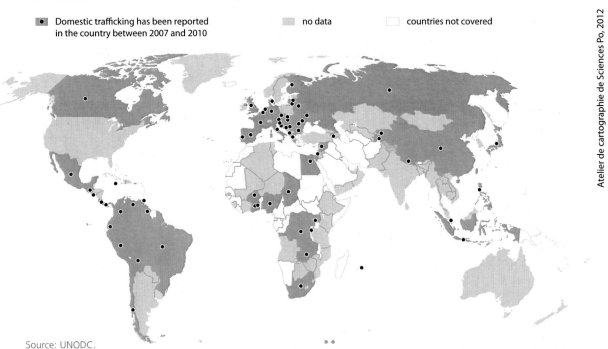

- ● Domestic trafficking has been reported in the country between 2007 and 2010
- no data
- countries not covered

Atelier de cartographie de Sciences Po, 2012

Source: UNODC.

25 Article 3, paragraph (a), of the Trafficking in Persons Protocol defines trafficking in persons as the recruitment, transportation, transfer, harbouring or receipt of persons, by different means for the purpose of exploitation.

26 In 2007, 40 countries reported about the nationality of the victims, with 24 of them reporting a total of about 1,100 victims of domestic trafficking. In 2008, 60 countries reported about the nationality of the victims, with 37 of those countries reporting a total of about 1,800 victims of domestic trafficking. In 2009, 62 countries reported about the nationality of the victims, with 41 of those countries reporting a total of about 2,100 victims of domestic trafficking. In 2010, 63 countries reported about the nationality of the victims, with 45 of those countries reporting a total of 2,200 victims of domestic trafficking.

FIG. 24: **Evolution of the prevalence of domestic trafficking between 2007 and 2010**

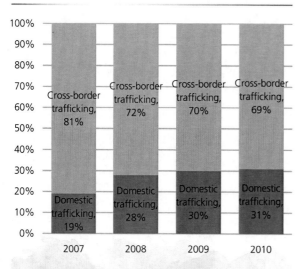

Source: UNODC elaboration of national data.

people in those countries are becoming more aware of the risks connected with certain migration paths. Thus, local traffickers may revert to local citizens, particularly groups who are vulnerable due to their young age, gender, ethnolinguistic background or socioeconomic situation.

The relevance of and increase in the detection of domestic trafficking around the world often reflect the different social and criminal contexts in the various countries. In some cases, they mirror socioeconomic differences within a society. Internal trafficking in China, for example, may reflect the massive internal migration from the rural areas to the fast-developing industrialized zones of the coasts. In the Philippines, a large share of victims domestically trafficked are exploited in child labour. A similar situation can be found in Ghana, where children are exploited in the Lake Volta fishing industry. Domestic trafficking in Europe may include the involvement of "loverboys", who manipulate their teenage girlfriends and lovers into exploitation in prostitution. This phenomenon has been widely documented in the Netherlands for years and is now being detected and reported in many other European countries. Similarly, a large share of domestic trafficking in Canada takes place for the purpose of sexual exploitation of girls between the ages of 14 and 25. These examples show that domestic trafficking happens in many ways and that it changes according to the country where it takes place.

Similar caveats to those discussed in the section about

other and new forms of exploitation apply here, however. An increasing number of internal trafficking cases recorded by local law enforcement agencies may simply represent a different way of categorizing certain crimes. It is likely that national jurisdictions around the world are expanding the applicability of the definition of trafficking in persons to certain exploitative situations that have always existed but were in the past categorized under other offences (sexual exploitation, forced labour, slavery and others). These cases may now be recorded as cases of trafficking in persons of own nationals within the country concerned. In this sense, the increasing number of detected victims of internal trafficking may be partly due to this evolution of national jurisprudence rather than an increase in the actual phenomenon.

To conclude, this section shows that most human trafficking is intraregional, and each region and subregion experiences specific and mostly geographically-characterized human trafficking flows in terms of origins and destinations. Similarly, the previous section on human trafficking patterns at the global level indicated that the different regions were affected by different types of trafficking in persons in terms of the profile of the victims and the traffickers as well as the forms of exploitation.

For that reason, the analysis of human trafficking patterns and flows needs to be completed through more specific and detailed regional insights.

Core results: global baseline on trafficking flows

- Victims of 136 different nationalities were detected in 118 countries between 2007 and 2010.

- About 460 different trafficking flows were identified between 2007 and 2010.

- Between 2007 and 2010, almost half of the victims detected worldwide were trafficked from a country within the same region as the country of destination. Twenty-four per cent of detected cases were part of a transcontinental trafficking flow.

- Domestic trafficking accounted for 27 per cent of the total global number of victims of trafficking in persons, and it was increasingly detected between 2007 and 2010.

- Western and Central Europe, North and Central America and the Middle East are the subregions where long distance trafficking is more frequently directed.

- The Middle East is the region reporting the highest share of victims trafficked from other regions of the world (70 per cent). Western and Central Europe display the largest geographic variety of trafficking origins, as 110 different nationalities from all the regions and subregions considered in this report were detected in that subregion.

- Between 2007 and 2010, the trafficking flow originating in East Asia continued to be the most prominent transnational flow at the global level. East Asian victims were detected in large numbers in many countries around the world.

- Victims from Eastern Europe and Central Asia as well as South America were detected in a wide number of countries within and outside their own regions. These trafficking flows do not appear to be very severe outside the regions of origin of the victims.

- Human trafficking originating in Africa has a severe connotation geographically limited to Africa, the Middle East and Western Europe.

CHAPTER II
PATTERNS AND FLOWS OF
TRAFFICKING IN PERSONS:
REGIONAL OVERVIEWS

Following the global overview, this chapter will focus on the four macroregions used in this report for a closer look at some of the salient regional information concerning trafficking patterns and flows. The order of presentation of the regions was determined by the size of the sample used for the analysis. Thus, the region of Europe and Central Asia, with solid country-level data coverage and the highest number of victims detected during the reporting period, is presented first.

A. EUROPE AND CENTRAL ASIA

Information from 48 countries in Europe and Central Asia was considered for the preparation of this report. Of these, 37 countries belong to the Western and Central Europe subregion, and 11 to the Eastern Europe and Central Asia subregion. Countries did not necessarily provide information for all indicators. The data coverage is solid and the sample size large enough to enable relatively detailed analyses of both subregions. Moreover, given the strong data, for this region it is also possible to present some cautious trend information regarding victim detections and trafficking flows.

1. Victims of trafficking in Europe and Central Asia

Thirty-two countries in Western and Central Europe reported the profile of about 22,000 victims detected in this subregion. In Eastern Europe and Central Asia, eight countries provided information on the profile of about 4,000 victims officially detected during the years considered by this report (2007-2010).

Adult women were the most frequently detected victims of trafficking in persons in Europe and Central Asia, as in the rest of the world. For the reporting period, the regional figures show an overall share of adult women of around 64 per cent of the total number of victims detected. Child trafficking accounts for 16 per cent of the victims detected in the whole region, while the share of adult men remains in the range of 19 per cent.

Adult women account for a share of about 80 per cent of the total victims detected in Eastern Europe and Central

FIG. 25: **Victims detected in Europe and Central Asia, by gender and age profile,** 2007-2010

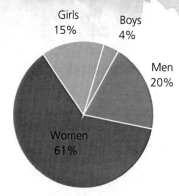

Western and Central Europe

Girls 15%
Boys 4%
Men 20%
Women 61%

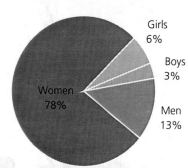

Eastern Europe and Central Asia

Girls 6%
Boys 3%
Men 13%
Women 78%

Source: UNODC elaboration of national data.

Asia, while in Western and Central Europe, this percentage is somewhat above 60 per cent. At the same time, the share of girls is some 10 per cent higher in Western and Central Europe than in Eastern Europe and Central Asia. About three of four child victims detected in Western and Central Europe are girls.

The overall share of children detected among the victims in Europe and Central Asia is the lowest compared with other regions of the world. Child trafficking accounts for about 20 per cent of the total number of victims in West-

FIG. 26: **Share of women prosecuted and convicted of trafficking, Eastern Europe and Central Asia, 2007-2010**

Prosecutions in Eastern Europe and Central Asia, 2007-2010

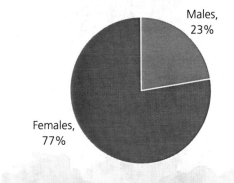

Males, 38%

Females, 62%

Convictions in Eastern Europe and Central Asia, 2007-2010

Males, 23%

Females, 77%

Source: UNODC elaboration of national data.

ern Europe, while it accounts for about 10 per cent in Eastern Europe and Central Asia.

The number of detected cases of child trafficking has increased somewhat in Europe and Central Asia in the past few years, however. In Western and Central Europe, the share of detected child victims increased from 17 to 19 per cent, and in Eastern Europe, it increased from 7 to 10 per cent between 2007 and 2010. Furthermore, compared with the 2003-2006 period, 15 countries in the region reported a clear increase in the share of child victims detected, with only 7 countries reporting a decreasing trend. For the rest of the countries it was not possible to identify trends regarding the profile of the victims for the whole reporting period.

Adult men were the second most frequently detected group of victims in Europe and Central Asia. Further-

more, Western and Central Europe registered a share of men among the total number of victims above the world average, at about 20 per cent.

2. Traffickers in Europe and Central Asia

As a large number of countries in this region provided data, it is possible to develop a relatively solid understanding of the profile of the offenders. The gender of those prosecuted for trafficking in persons was reported by 28 countries, while 30 reported on persons convicted.

Countries in Eastern Europe and Central Asia report very high rates of female participation in trafficking in persons-related crimes — above 50 per cent — with peaks above 70 per cent in the Southern Caucasus. This high rate is constant for the whole period and is similar to what was reported in the *Global Report on Trafficking in Persons* of 2009.[27] Most victims in the region are women trafficked for sexual exploitation, which is the form of trafficking in which female traffickers are particularly involved. However, the high rate of female involvement cannot be explained by the profile of the victims alone. A law enforcement focus largely limited to lower-ranking segments of the trafficking network — where women are more likely to be found — could be another explanatory factor, though additional research would be needed to explain why.

Authorities in the rest of Europe report — in line with the global results — that there is a higher participation of women in human trafficking than in other crimes. The regional average share of women convicted of trafficking is about 23 per cent of the total; for prosecutions, the share is the same.

Countries report very different proportions with regard to the gender profile of the offenders, however. Some countries report the same level of female participation in human trafficking as in other crimes. This group includes Croatia, Germany, Hungary, the Netherlands, Slovakia and the United Kingdom. As previously shown, female traffickers are more often involved in sexual exploitation. These low levels cannot be explained by a higher prevalence of trafficking for forced labour, as these countries register a relatively low number of these cases while, in relative terms, more frequently detecting sexual exploita-

27 *Global Report on Trafficking in Persons* (2009), p. 47; available at www. unodc.org/glotip.

FIG. 27: **Share of women convicted of trafficking in persons (2007-2010) and of all crimes (2006-2009), selected countries in Europe and Central Asia**

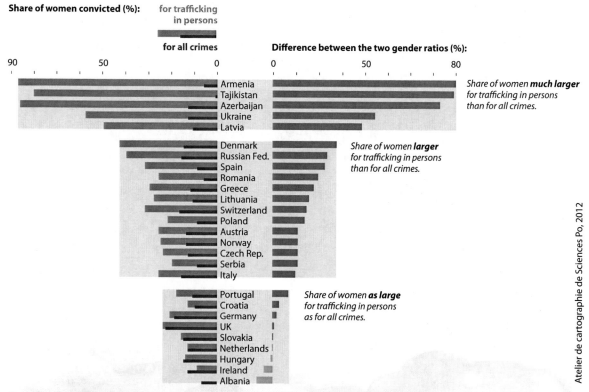

Source: UNODC, elaboration of national data and the United Nations Survey of Crime Trends and Operations of Criminal Justice Systems.

tion. This suggests that the participation of women in trafficking in persons for sexual exploitation is not only connected with the profile of the victims but also to certain characteristics of criminal networks operating in different countries.

In Western and Central Europe, the percentage of individuals convicted of trafficking in persons that were women ranged between 50 per cent in Latvia to none in Albania. Qualitative studies show that Albanian trafficking networks are generally male-driven,[28] which explains the fact that only men are convicted of human trafficking in that country. While some sex trafficking rings employ women traffickers, others may not.

As far as the nationality of the offenders is concerned, in Europe, more foreign nationals are convicted of traffick-

ing in persons than of other crimes. As mentioned above, the fact that trafficking mainly targets migrants means that more frequent involvement of foreign residents in this crime may reasonably be expected.

Similar to other regions, the relevance of foreign traffickers is higher in destination countries, where victims are exploited. In Europe, this means that Western Europe, which is largely a destination subregion for human trafficking, has a relatively high rate of involvement of foreign nationals.

3. Forms of exploitation in Europe and Central Asia

For this report, 37 countries reported information regarding the forms of exploitation of more than 27,000 victims detected between 2007 and 2010 (or more recently). Of them, 7 countries are in Eastern Europe and Central Asia (about 6,500 victims) and 30 countries are in Western and Central Europe (about 20,600 victims).

••
28 *The Trafficking Flows and Routes of Eastern Europe* (WEST Project, 2005); R. Surtees, "Traffickers and Trafficking in Southern and Eastern Europe", *European Journal of Criminology*, volume 5 (1) (2008), pp. 39-68.

FIG. 28: **Share of foreign nationals convicted of trafficking in persons (2007-2010) and for all crimes (2006-2009), selected countries in Europe and Central Asia**

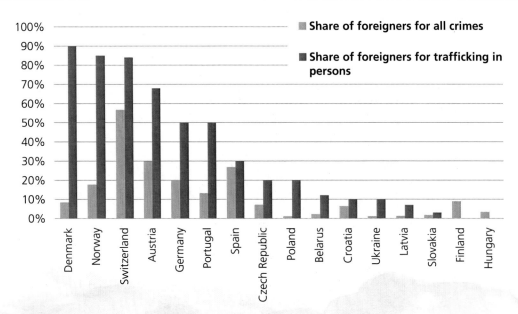

■ **Share of foreigners for all crimes**

■ **Share of foreigners for trafficking in persons**

Source: UNODC, elaboration of national data and the United Nations Survey of Crime Trends and Operations of Criminal Justice Systems.

Compared with other regions, Europe and Central Asia reported more cases of trafficking for sexual exploitation than for purposes of forced labour. During the reporting period, the share of victims trafficked for forced labour, slavery and servitude was 31 per cent of the victims detected in the region, while about 62 per cent of victims were trafficked for sexual exploitation. When comparing the two subregions that comprise this region, it appears that trafficking for forced labour is more prevalent in Eastern Europe and Central Asia (35 per cent) than in Western and Central Europe (29 per cent). When trafficking for forced labour was detected in Western and Central Europe, victims were generally exploited in the agriculture, construction or catering sectors.

Exploitation of trafficking victims as domestic workers was also reported in Western and Central Europe. In particular, Austria reported a relatively large number of trafficking victims in domestic servitude: about 15 per cent of the victims assisted by the local non-governmental organization LEFÖ between 2007 and 2010. In the Netherlands, these victims accounted for about 2 per cent of the total victims assisted by CoMensha, a non-governmental organization, between 2007 and 2009. Trafficking for domestic servitude was also documented in the Czech

FIG. 29: **Distribution of forms of exploitation detected in Europe and Central Asia, 2007-2010**

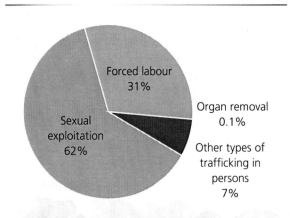

Source: UNODC elaboration of national data.

Republic and in some other Western and Central European countries.

The share of victims trafficked for purposes not specified in the Trafficking in Persons Protocol was in the range of 7 per cent. In Western and Central Europe, the number of victims of trafficking for the purpose of begging was about 2 per cent of the total detected victims. Instances of child trafficking for begging and for the purpose of committing petty crimes have been reported in eight countries in Western and Central Europe, mainly in the Balkans, but it was also detected in Belgium, Italy, the Netherlands, Norway and Slovakia. Trafficking in children for begging or for the purpose of committing crime was also detected in the Republic of Moldova and Ukraine. Azerbaijan and Bulgaria reported cases of the sale of babies, and Portugal reported cases of trafficking for illegal adoption. Episodes of trafficking for forced marriages were documented in Austria, Croatia and Serbia. Cases of trafficking for exploitation in pornography were also documented in Belgium and Romania.

Human trafficking for organ removal was reported by five countries in West and Central Europe and three in Eastern and Central Asia, although the proportion of such cases (0.1 per cent) was limited in relation to the total number of victims trafficked for any purpose. Nonetheless, the geographical scope of these detections shows that this phenomenon should not be underestimated in Europe.

4. Trafficking flows in Europe and Central Asia

For the purpose of this report, 32 countries in Western and Central Europe reported the nationality of about 16,800 victims detected between 2007 and 2010 (or more recently).

As reported in the global overview of the trafficking flows (section I.B.1), Western and Central Europe is a destination of trafficking in persons of a wide range of origins. Western and Central European countries reported trafficking flows originating in more than 110 origin countries in all regions of the world. Clearly, not all the detected trafficking flows have the same relevance. Origin areas within the subregion play a major role, as does domestic trafficking.

From another perspective, this also means that this region has a significant role in terms of origin of trafficking. Trafficking originating in Western and Central Europe remains nearly exclusively confined to this subregion. During the reporting period, only 35 victims that were nationals of Western and Central European countries were detected

MAP 12: **Origin of victims trafficked to Western and Central Europe, share of the total number of victims detected there,** 2007-2010

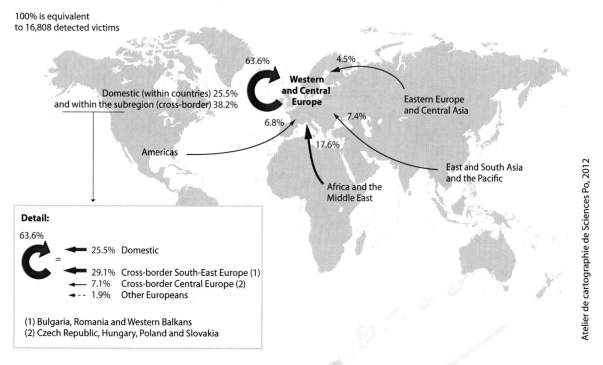

100% is equivalent to 16,808 detected victims

63.6%   4.5%

Western and Central Europe

Domestic (within countries) 25.5% and within the subregion (cross-border) 38.2%

Eastern Europe and Central Asia

6.8%   7.4%

Americas

17.6%

East and South Asia and the Pacific

Africa and the Middle East

Detail:

63.6%

= 25.5% Domestic
29.1% Cross-border South-East Europe (1)
7.1% Cross-border Central Europe (2)
1.9% Other Europeans

(1) Bulgaria, Romania and Western Balkans
(2) Czech Republic, Hungary, Poland and Slovakia

Atelier de cartographie de Sciences Po, 2012

Source: UNODC.

outside the subregion, which suggests that flows originating in Western and Central Europe are generally of short range. Moreover, some 25 per cent of the victims detected in Western and Central Europe between 2007 and 2010 were exploited in their own countries.

A more detailed analysis of trafficking originating in Europe shows that trafficking in the subregion frequently involves victims from countries of South-Eastern Europe (also part of the Western and Central Europe subregion) trafficked to almost all European countries covered by the report.

Romanian and Bulgarian victims were detected in a large number of countries in Western and Central Europe. Victims from the Western Balkans (mainly Albanians, Bosnians and Serbians) were also detected, although less frequently. In total, victims from the Balkan area accounted for about 30 per cent of the victims detected in Western and Central Europe during the reporting period.

Nationals of countries in South-Eastern Europe are not the only European victims of trafficking detected, however. During the reporting period, victims from the Czech Republic, Hungary, Poland and Slovakia — here categorized as the "Central European countries" — were detected in this subregion. These nationals accounted for 7 per cent of the total victims detected in Western and Central Europe.

Victims from Eastern Europe and Central Asia were widely detected in Western and Central Europe during the reporting period, albeit in small numbers. Victims from the subregion were detected in or repatriated from 32 Western and Central European countries, for a total of about 5 per cent of the total number of victims detected in those countries. As discussed below, when considering trends over time, victims from Eastern Europe and Central Asia appear to be detected in decreasing numbers in Western and Central Europe, suggesting a reduction of this trafficking flow in recent years.

Notwithstanding the prominence of intraregional European trafficking, Western and Central Europe is clearly also a destination for a large number of trafficking victims originating in other regions. Between 2007 and 2010 (or more recently, when available), Western and Central European countries have detected more than 70 different nationalities of victims trafficked from Africa and the Middle East, the Americas and South Asia, East Asia and the Pacific.

Of the victims originating outside Europe, those from African countries are most prominently detected. About 18 per cent of the total number of victims detected in Western and Central Europe are African. Victims from West Africa, especially but not only Nigerians, comprise the vast majority. West Africans accounted for about 14 per cent of the total number of victims detected here, and they were reported by 20 countries of Western and Central European. West Africans were detected in the Scandinavian countries, Austria, Belgium, France, Germany, Greece, Ireland, Italy, the Netherlands, Spain, the United Kingdom and other countries.

In terms of trends, the proportion of West African victims among the total number of victims detected remained constant in Western and Central Europe during the reporting period. A detailed analysis at the country level, however, shows that a decreasing number of West African victims have been detected in a series of countries, while an increasing number have been detected in others. During the reporting period, fewer West African victims were detected in France and Italy, while they were increasingly detected in Austria and Germany. Similar contrasting trends can be noted among other destination countries in Western and Central Europe. The aggregated regional value is the result of compensation between opposite trends. This may indicate that the West African trafficking flow within the subregion may face some sort of displacement of destination.

Victims from the rest of sub-Saharan Africa accounted for a little more than 1 per cent of all victims detected in Western and Central Europe. As far as the North African victims are concerned, these were detected in or repatriated from 11 European countries, accounting for about 2.5 per cent of the victims detected during the reporting period, suggesting that these flows should not be underestimated.

Victims from East Asia accounted for about 7 per cent of those detected between 2007 and 2010 in Western and Central Europe. East Asian victims were reported by authorities of 16 countries in this subregion, from Scandinavia to Central Europe, the Mediterranean area and the United Kingdom, showing a wide diffusion of these trafficking flows within Western and Central Europe. The share of victims from South Asia detected in the subregion accounted for just over 1 per cent of the total, and victims from South Asia were reported by 13 Western and Central European countries during the reporting period.

Victims from the Americas accounted for about 7 per cent of the total number of victims detected in Western and

Central Europe, almost all from South America and the Caribbean. A large share of these victims were trafficked to Spain, although the trafficking originating in the Americas involved 19 destination countries in this part of Europe, including Belgium, Denmark, France, the Netherlands, Portugal and Switzerland, as well as Cyprus, the Czech Republic and Romania. Thus, the data display a wide diffusion within Western and Central Europe of the human trafficking flow out of the Americas.

For the purpose of this report, seven countries in Eastern Europe and Central Asia reported the nationality of about 2,460 victims detected between 2007 and 2010 (or more recently). These countries present different characteristics in terms of human trafficking flows compared with Western and Central Europe.

As a destination of human trafficking, the vast majority of the victims of trafficking detected in Eastern Europe and Central Asia are nationals of countries within the subregion. With respect to victims trafficked from other regions during the reporting period, victims have been reported to be trafficked from East Asia to this subregion. Owing to the lack of solid statistics, it is not possible to estimate the severity of this trafficking flow, however.

In terms of origins of human trafficking, when Eastern European and Central Asian nationals were trafficked outside the subregion, they were more frequently detected in Western and Central Europe or the Middle East. Nationals of Eastern Europe and Central Asia were also detected in Asia and the Americas.

Nationals of Eastern Europe and Central Asia were detected in or repatriated from 32 countries in Western and Central Europe during the reporting period, which indicates that this trafficking flow is widely dispersed. Victims from this subregion were detected in most parts of Europe, including Cyprus, Greece and Turkey, and also in Austria, Germany and the Netherlands as well as in the Scandinavian countries, the Mediterranean area, Central Europe and the Balkans. In addition, there is not just one or only a few highly predominant countries of origin of this trafficking flow. Eastern European victims (mainly Moldovans, Russians and Ukrainians) were detected in a wide range of countries in Western and Central Europe, and trafficking involving Central Asians (nationals of Kyrgyzstan, Turkmenistan and Uzbekistan) was also reported in the subregion. A limited number of nationals from countries in the Southern Caucasus were also detected in Western and Central Europe.

Another destination for victims originating in Eastern Europe and Central Asia is the Middle East, where they

MAP 13: **Destinations of trafficked Eastern Europeans and Central Asians, as a proportion of the total number of victims detected at specific destinations, 2007-2010**

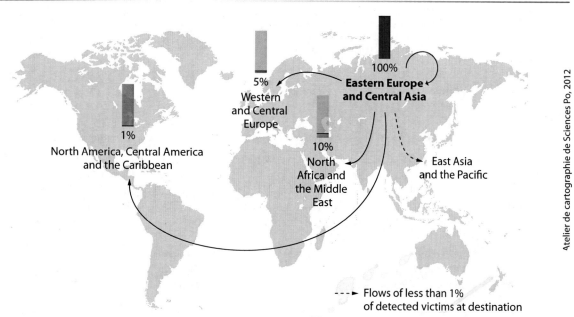

Source: UNODC.

account for about 10 per cent of the total number of victims detected. Central Asian victims were detected in the Gulf countries of the Middle East. Victims from Eastern Europe were detected in or repatriated from other parts of the Middle East.

During the reporting period, victims from Eastern Europe and Central Asia were also detected in South-East Asia, as well as in North and Central America, albeit in limited numbers.

When considering trends over a longer time period, it appears that the trafficking flows from Eastern Europe and Central Asia have been declining. An analysis in that regard can be conducted by considering a selected number of destination countries providing solid data on the nationality of the victims detected over a longer reporting period. Most of the countries in Western and Central Europe, an important destination for victims of these nationalities, report a generally decreasing number and share of Eastern European and Central Asian victims among those detected between 2000 and 2010.

When considering the aggregated data for victims originating in Eastern Europe and Central Asia that were detected in all of Western and Central Europe during the reporting period, the proportion of such nationals among

the total number of victims decreased from 14 per cent in 2007 to 5 per cent in 2009, and decreased even further in 2010. A similar trend can be noted in the other important destination for these victims, the Middle East, although the data from that subregion are less solid.

Worldwide, some 18 countries registered a clearly decreasing share of victims from Eastern Europe and Central Asia among the victims detected during the reporting period. A slight increase was noted in France (from 2 to 3 per cent). In Indonesia, nationals of countries of that subregion were detected for the first time in 2010. There is no evidence of any increase in victims from Eastern Europe and Central Asia being trafficked in North America.

The lack of reliable time series data in other regions of the world does not permit conclusive statements regarding whether the declining trend is limited to the destinations considered in this analysis, or whether it is a general reduction of the trafficking out of this subregion. It is possible that these flows have been displaced to other regions or to countries where information is not available for a range of years, for instance in South-East Asia or in Central America, where these nationals have been episodically detected. However, there are indications that trafficking originating in Eastern Europe and Central Asia with destinations in other parts of the world is decreasing overall.

FIG. 30: **Share of Eastern European and Central Asian victims among all victims detected in selected countries in Western and Central Europe, 2000-2010**

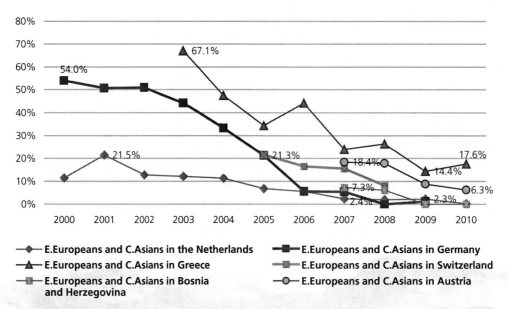

Source: UNODC elaboration of national data.

FIG. 31: **Proportion of Eastern European and Central Asian victims among all victims assisted in Dubai (United Arab Emirates) and in Israel, 2008-2010**

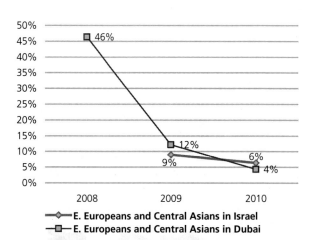

Source: UNODC elaboration of national data.

Core results: patterns and flows in Europe and Central Asia

* During the period considered, a large proportion of the victims detected were adult women, while children accounted for 16 per cent of the total, and girls were more frequently trafficked than boys. Child trafficking in Europe and Central Asia increased slightly during the reporting period.

* During the reporting period, 62 per cent of the victims detected in Europe and Central Asia were trafficked for sexual exploitation, and 31 per cent for forced labour.

* Trafficking for "other forms of exploitation" accounted for 7 per cent of the victims detected between 2007 and 2010 (or more recently). Among these forms, child begging was the form most commonly detected (about 2 per cent).

* The share of women prosecuted and convicted of the crime of trafficking in persons was relatively high in Eastern Europe and Central Asia during the years considered.

* Between 2007 and 2010, countries in Western and Central Europe reported a large share of victims (63 per cent) who had been trafficked within the subregion in either cross-border or domestic trafficking. In the subregion, one victim in four is trafficked domestically.

* The most common origin of victims of cross-border trafficking in Western and Central Europe is the Balkans. Other significant areas of origins of trafficking victims detected in the subregion are West Africa, East Asia and the Americas.

* During the reporting period, countries in Eastern Europe and Central Asia almost exclusively reported victims who had originated in the same subregion. At the same time, victims from the subregion were detected in significant numbers in Western Europe and the Middle East.

* There are indications that trafficking from Eastern Europe and Central Asia to other parts of the world is generally decreasing.

B. THE AMERICAS

Information from 27 countries of the Americas was considered for the preparation of this report. Of these, 17 countries are in North America, Central America and the Caribbean, and 10 countries belong to the South American subregion. Countries did not necessarily provide information for all indicators. The data coverage in this region is relatively solid, and the sample size is large enough to permit relatively detailed analysis of both subregions.

1. Victims of trafficking in the Americas

The profile of the victims detected in the Americas can vary greatly from country to country. Fifteen countries of this region provided information about the profile of more than 6,000 victims of trafficking in persons detected between 2007 and 2010 (or more recently). Of these victims, about 1,600 were children, accounting for about 27 per cent of the total number of victims detected in the region.

While all forms of trafficking exist in the Americas, it is difficult to identify a common profile of the victims reported by the countries covered by this report.

A large part of the trafficking victims reported by the national authorities in the Americas were females, both adult women and girls. Countries of the region reported a limited number of male victims. Some countries report a large proportion of girls among the victims, while other countries most frequently detect adult women.

Similarly, the extent of child trafficking in this region differs significantly according to the countries involved.

FIG. 32: **Victims of trafficking in the Americas, by age group, 2007-2010**

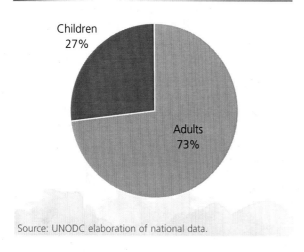

Source: UNODC elaboration of national data.

During the reporting period, in South America, the Southern Cone countries detected and reported a large share of adults among the victims. Conversely, the northern part of South America as well as Central America detected more children among the victims than adults; shares of child trafficking were above the regional average.

FIG. 33: **Victims of trafficking in selected countries in the Americas, by age group, 2007-2010**

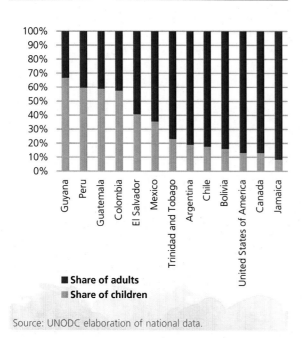

■ Share of adults
■ Share of children

Source: UNODC elaboration of national data.

FIG. 34: **Detected child trafficking trends in selected countries in the Americas, 2007-2011**

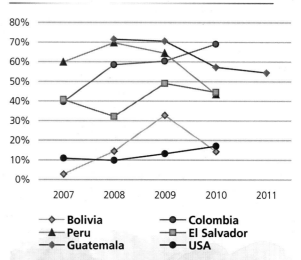

◆ **Bolivia**   ● **Colombia**
▲ **Peru**   ■ **El Salvador**
◆ **Guatemala**   ● **USA**

Source: UNODC elaboration of national data.

An increasing proportion of children were among the detected victims in some countries of the region, including Colombia, El Salvador, the United States and, until 2009, the Plurinational State of Bolivia. However, this trend is not representative of the entire region, as some other countries, such as Guatemala and Peru, recorded a decreasing trend in the share of child victims detected during the reporting period.

2. Traffickers in the Americas

Nine countries in the Americas provided data on the gender profile of persons prosecuted for trafficking in persons, and 13 countries provided that information for those convicted. According to those data, the level of participation of women in human trafficking in the region is higher than the world average: about 50 per cent of persons prosecuted for human trafficking are females.

It appears that in this region women who are prosecuted for trafficking in persons are less likely than men to be convicted: women constitute a relatively low 35 per cent of offenders convicted of human trafficking.

In line with observations with respect to other regions and the global situation, the female offending ratio for trafficking in persons is higher than for other crimes. In the Americas, women rarely comprise less than 20 per cent of convictions for all crimes.

FIG. 35: **Proportion of women prosecuted for trafficking in persons in selected countries of North, Central and South America, as a percentage of all trafficking prosecutions, 2007-2010**

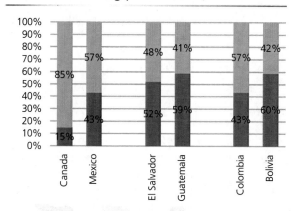

■ Share of females prosecuted ■ Share of males prosecuted

Source: UNODC elaboration of national data.

FIG. 36: **Proportion of foreign nationals among those convicted of trafficking in persons (2007-2010) and of all crimes (2006-2009), selected countries**

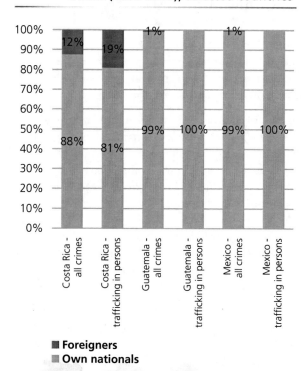

■ Foreigners
■ Own nationals

Source: UNODC elaboration on national data and Crime Trends Survey data.

Among the countries providing this type of information, the only exception is Canada, where the proportion of women prosecuted for trafficking in persons is very low compared with the rest of the world and is lower than the proportion of women convicted of other crimes. In some countries, for example, in the Andean region and Central America, there are more women prosecuted or convicted for trafficking in persons than men.

The 10 countries of this region that reported the nationality of offenders did not report any significant differences between the profiles of those convicted of trafficking and those convicted of other crimes. The average percentage of those convicted of trafficking in persons who are foreign nationals is about 4 per cent, while Canada reports only Canadian offenders among its few convicts.

3. Forms of exploitation in the Americas

Form of exploitation was reported for more than 3,700 victims detected by 17 countries in the Americas between 2007 and 2010 (or more recently). When the whole region is considered, trafficking in persons for sexual exploitation was more frequently reported than other forms of trafficking (51 per cent of the total number of victims). However, the share of victims trafficked for forced labour is significant (44 per cent), indicating that this form of trafficking, as detected, is proportionately higher in the Americas than in Europe and Central Asia.

In addition, the regional figures do not take into account the large share of victims detected by the authorities in South America as being "under slavery conditions", because the figure reported also includes persons working under degrading or substandard conditions. Thus, this distribution is likely to underestimate the proportion of trafficking for forced labour vis-à-vis sexual exploitation in the Americas.[29]

Countries of North America reported a large percentage of victims who were trafficked for forced labour. In the United States, the share of victims trafficked for forced labour accounted for more than 70 per cent of the total number of victims detected during the reporting period, while in Mexico, the share of forced labour was more than 65 per cent of the total. Canada also recorded an increas-

••
29 These figures do not include victims of slavery or degrading working conditions, as it was not specified how many of these victims were due to trafficking. For detailed information about these countries see the country profiles.

FIG. 37: **Distribution of forms of exploitation detected in the Americas, 2007-2010**

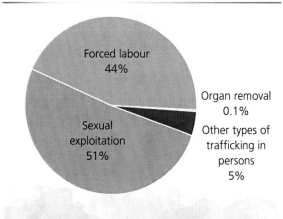

Source: UNODC elaboration of national data.

ing number of victims of trafficking for forced labour involving foreign nationals, although the 2010 Royal Canadian Mounted Police assessment[30] identified trafficking for sexual exploitation as the prevailing type of trafficking in persons in the country.

Between 2007 and 2010, the countries of Central America and the Caribbean reported very high proportions of victims trafficked for sexual exploitation. The number of cases of trafficking for forced labour was limited.

South American countries reported more cases of trafficking for sexual exploitation than for other forms of exploitation. At the same time, the number of detected victims who were trafficked for forced labour was significant. The Plurinational State of Bolivia reported that about 42 per cent of the victims detected during the years considered were exploited in labour activities, while the corresponding share was 37 per cent in Argentina and 39 per cent in Chile. The authorities in Ecuador detected victims of trafficking for forced labour, slavery and servitude.

Moreover, among judicial or extrajudicial proceedings, Brazilian authorities identified some 5,000 persons in slavery-like or degrading working conditions during the period considered.

During the reporting period, the Andean countries (Colombia, Ecuador, Peru and the Plurinational State of Bolivia) reported instances of forced marriages and traf-

ficking for begging or to commit crime. Some of the Andean countries also reported cases of trafficking for illegal adoption and selling of babies, and the authorities of Ecuador reported forced recruitment into armed forces in 2008. Trafficking for illegal adoptions was reported by the authorities of El Salvador, while the United Nations Stabilization Mission in Haiti (MINUSTAH) reported cases of cross-border illegal adoption in Haiti in 2009. Moreover, some cases of trafficking for organ removal have been reported in South and North America.

4. Trafficking flows in the Americas

Trafficking in the Americas is largely intraregional. Most of the victims detected in the Americas between 2007 and 2010 were nationals of countries in this region and were either trafficked domestically or across borders to another country within the region. The relevance of geographical proximity is also confirmed at the subregional level. Most of the South American countries are detecting South American victims, while most of the victims detected in North and Central America are Central Americans or people from the Caribbean. As far as interregional trafficking flows are concerned, the data collected indicates that a significant number of East Asian victims were trafficked into the Americas, and some South American victims were trafficked into Western and Central Europe.

From the point of view of destination countries, during the period covered by this report, 18 countries in the Americas reported the nationality of more than 2,400 victims trafficked and detected in the region.

As in other parts of the world, the trafficking flows within the region follow the general pattern of victims trafficked from the relatively poorer to the comparatively richer neighbouring countries. A large proportion of the regional victims detected in the United States are Mexicans, Central Americans and people from Caribbean countries. Most of the victims detected in Mexico are Guatemalan, whereas Guatemala reported mainly detecting victims from El Salvador and Nicaragua, and El Salvador detected victims from its neighbouring countries.

A similar situation is found in South America, where, for example, victims originating in the Plurinational State of Bolivia have been detected in Brazil, Chile and Peru. In Chile, victims from Brazil, Ecuador, Paraguay and Peru were detected. Victims from the Plurinational State of Bolivia and Ecuador were reported in Peru.

During the reporting period, South American victims

---

30 Royal Canadian Mounted Police, *Human Trafficking in Canada: A Threat Assessment* (2010), available at www.rcmp-grc.gc.ca/pubs/ht-tp/htta-tpem-eng.htm.

FIG. 38: **Gross domestic product per capita of selected countries in the Americas, 2010**

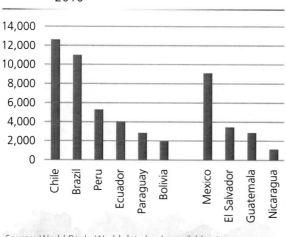

Source: World Bank, World data bank, available at http://databank.worldbank.org/ddp/home.do.

accounted for about 3 per cent of the victims detected in North and Central America and the Caribbean. During the same period, about 1.5 per cent of the victims of trafficking reported by South American countries were nationals of Central America and the Caribbean. Considering also that each country has a large number of victims trafficked domestically, it seems that most of the trafficking

in the Americas takes place within the subregion of origin.

Nevertheless, one of every five trafficking victims detected in the Americas during the reporting period was a national of a country in East Asia. That trafficking flow was found not only in North America but also in Central and South American countries. During the reporting period, East Asian victims were detected in or repatriated from 13 countries in the Americas — a wide variety of destinations given the large geographical size of the region. In terms of severity, East Asians accounted for 27 per cent of the victims detected in North America, Central America and the Caribbean and for 10 per cent of the victims detected in South America. A significant number of Thais, Filipinos and other East Asian victims were detected in the United States and, to a lesser extent, Canada. A smaller number of Chinese victims were detected in Chile, Colombia, Ecuador, Mexico and Venezuela (Bolivarian Republic of); some Vietnamese and other East Asian nationals were trafficked to Costa Rica; and a limited number of victims from East Asia were also reported in El Salvador and countries in the Caribbean. Thus, the data indicate that there is a significant trafficking flow from East Asia to the Americas, both in terms of the number of victims detected and the diffusion of the trafficking flows to different destination areas of the region.

MAP 14: **Origin of victims trafficked to North America, Central America and the Caribbean, as proportion of the total number of victims detected in the subregion, 2007-2010**

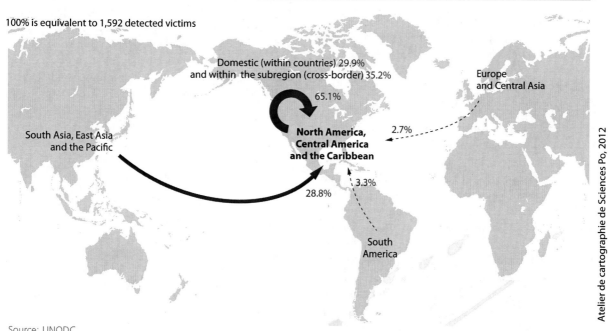

Source: UNODC.

MAP 15: **Origin of victims trafficked to South America, as proportion of the total number of victims detected in the subregion, 2007-2010**

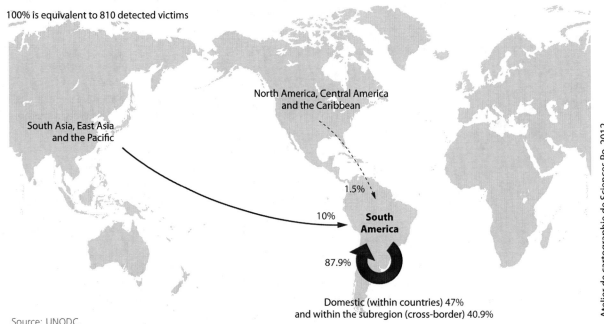

100% is equivalent to 810 detected victims

North America, Central America and the Caribbean

South Asia, East Asia and the Pacific

1.5%

10%

South America

87.9%

Domestic (within countries) 47% and within the subregion (cross-border) 40.9%

Source: UNODC.

Atelier de cartographie de Sciences Po, 2012

As far as the other regions of origin, victims from Europe have been detected in North America but rarely elsewhere in the Americas. Similarly, South Asian victims have been detected in the United States but rarely in other countries in the region. Some episodes involving African victims were also reported in this region during the period considered.

From the point of view of the origin of victims, victims from the Americas were either detected in or repatriated as victims of trafficking from 50 countries around the world. As already discussed, most of the destinations identified were within the region.

With respect to destinations outside the region, during the reporting period, South American victims were detected in Western and Central Europe, where they accounted for about 6 per cent of the total number of detected victims. Victims from Brazil, Colombia and Paraguay were particularly prominent in Spain, but they were also detected by authorities of other countries in Europe. Brazilian victims were detected in 12 countries in Western and Central Europe, and Colombians in eight. The Colombian authorities reported the repatriation of Colombian victims of trafficking in persons from some countries in East Asia. Episodes of trafficking of Brazilian and Colombian victims were also reported in Israel.

As for human trafficking flows originating in Central America and the Caribbean, the most prominent seems to be the flow from the Dominican Republic. Dominican victims have been detected in or repatriated from 18 countries around the world, mainly in the Americas and Europe. Between 2007 and 2010, Dominican victims accounted for about 1 per cent of the victims detected in Western and Central Europe, and about 3 per cent of the victims detected in the Americas. Within the region, Dominican victims were detected in South America, Central America and the Caribbean and the United States. Authorities in the United States also detected victims from Haiti.

MAP 16: **Destinations of trafficking victims originating in South America, as a proportion of the total number of victims detected at specific destinations, 2007-2010**

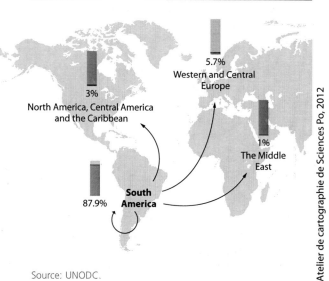

Source: UNODC.

MAP 17: **Destinations of trafficking victims originating in North America, Central America and the Caribbean, as a proportion of the total number of victims detected at specific destinations, 2007-2010**

Source: UNODC.

Core results: patterns and flows in the Americas

- A large majority of the victims detected in the Americas are female — either women or girls.

- Child trafficking accounts for about 27 per cent of the trafficking in the entire region and is more prominent in Central America and the northern part of South America. It has been increasingly detected in some countries of the region.

- During the reporting period, 51 per cent of the victims detected in the Americas were trafficked for sexual exploitation and 44 per cent for forced labour,[31] and forced labour is likely underrepresented.

- Most of the trafficking flows involving the Americas are intraregional. During the years considered, North and Central American countries mainly detected victims originating in North and Central America, while South American countries mainly detected victims originating in South America.

- East Asian victims accounted for more than 20 per cent of the total number of victims detected in this region. East Asian victims were widely detected in different countries across the Americas.

- During the reporting period, victims from South America, Central America and the Caribbean were also detected in significant numbers in Western and Central Europe and were less frequently detected in the Middle East and East Asia.

31 These figures do not include the large numbers of victims of slavery or degrading working conditions detected in South America. For detailed information about these countries please consult the country profiles, available at http://www.unodc.org/glotip.

Estimating the severity of trafficking

Trafficking in persons is a serious problem because it affects nearly all countries in the world and it imposes severe harm on victims of trafficking. We know that women, men and children are trafficked through hundreds of flows within countries, between countries, and using intra- and interregional trafficking routes. We know that traffickers are exploiting victims in many different ways and still many of the criminals walk free because the conviction rates are so low. Despite all our knowledge on human trafficking, estimating the severity of the problem remains a challenge.

Knowing the number of human trafficking cases or victims in different countries would indeed help to assess the severity of the problem. However, trafficking in persons is largely a hidden crime which rarely is reported to the authorities. Thus, it is impossible to measure the scale of trafficking in persons using only official criminal justice statistics even though they can provide valuable information on patterns and flows, as well as on how the police, prosecutors and courts respond to trafficking cases.

This Global Report is mainly based on official information on the national criminal justice responses to trafficking in persons. That is why the Report is not measuring the prevalence or severity of trafficking in persons globally, regionally or nationally. The Report focuses on the patterns and flows of trafficking in persons as requested by the General Assembly. In future Reports, other aspects of trafficking in persons may also be studied. The way forward for research on trafficking in persons is discussed in Chapter II.

During the last ten years, several different estimates have been presented on the number of victims of trafficking in persons globally. However, broad agreement has not been reached regarding which methods should be used to calculate such estimates. As a result, quoted figures sometimes contradict each other or indicate a very large range for the number of victims.

The most reliable estimates have been provided by the International Labour Organization (ILO) which has extensive experience in estimating the severity of forced labour. While there is a clear link between the Trafficking in Persons Protocol and the ILO Convention No. 29 [a], there are also differences in the conceptualization of trafficking in persons. The United Nations Trafficking in Persons Protocol defines forced labour as one form of trafficking in persons among other forms of exploitation. For ILO, human trafficking can be regarded as one form of forced labour among other forms of forced labour.

The first minimum estimate of victims of forced labour and trafficking in persons in the world was published by the ILO in 2005. This report presented estimates for the number of victims of forced labour, as well as a specific estimate for victims of trafficking in persons as one form of forced labour. According to this report, at least 12.3 million people were victims of forced labour worldwide and the estimated minimum number of persons in forced labour as a result of trafficking in persons was 2.45 million, at any moment in time [b]. In the same year, ILO published the first estimation of the global profits generated from the world's 2.45 million forced labourers who have been trafficked amounting to US$31.6 billion per year [c].

In 2012, on the basis of a more accurate methodology, ILO provided new figures on the number of victims of forced labour. The new estimates [d] are based on cases of forced labour reported by a variety of sources, including governmental and non governmental documents, reports from international organizations and from academia, ILO reports, documents from trade unions and employers' organizations, as well as media accounts. The cases considered needed to fulfill certain qualification criteria to be included in the analysis. These cases serve as a data on the basis of which an extrapolation methodology is used to derive the estimated number of victims of forced labour.

The ILO 2012 report estimates that there were 20.9 million victims of forced labour globally at any given time over the 2002-2011 period. Out of these victims, 9.1 million have moved internally or internationally, while 11.8 million are subject to forced labour in their place of origin or residence. ILO provides a breakdown of the types of forced labour that victims experienced (forced labour exploitation, forced sexual exploitation and state-imposed forced labour). A separate estimate on the number of victims of forced labour as a result of trafficking in persons was not derived. The estimated number of victims of forced labour includes also victims of trafficking in persons; however, the exact number of trafficking victims remains unknown.

a   The term forced or compulsory labour is defined in Article 2.1. as *all work or service which is exacted from any person under the menace of any penalty and for which the said person has not offered himself voluntarily.*

b   ILO, *A global alliance against forced labour.* Global Report under the Follow-up to the ILO Declaration of Fundamental Principles and Rights at Work. Report of the Director General. International Labour Conference 93rd Session 2005. Report I (B). International labour Organization: Geneva, 2005

c   Belser, Patrick, *Forced Labour and Human Trafficking: Estimating the Profits.* Working Paper 42. International Labour Office: Geneva, 2005

d   ILO, *ILO Global Estimate on Forced Labour: Results and Methodology,* Geneva, June 2012.

C. SOUTH ASIA, EAST ASIA AND THE PACIFIC

Information from 20 countries in South Asia, East Asia and the Pacific was considered for the preparation of this report. Of those, 5 countries belong to the South Asia subregion, and 15 countries belong to the subregion of East Asia and the Pacific. Countries did not necessarily provide information for all indicators. The data coverage in this region is relatively weak, especially in the light of the region's large population. As a result, while the sample size is relatively large compared with that of other subregions, there is a high degree of uncertainty regarding how representative it is of the actual trafficking situation.

1. Victims of trafficking in South Asia, East Asia and the Pacific

More than 10,000 cases of trafficking in persons have been recorded in South Asia, East Asia and the Pacific. However, a profile of the victims was available for a limited number of those cases. First and foremost, because the profile of the victims was not made available to UNODC, but also because these cases were often prosecuted under other offences, including victims of other crimes. Just nine[32] countries in this large region provided information concerning the profile of more than 3,800 victims of trafficking in persons detected between 2007 and 2010. As a consequence, the results of this regional analysis cannot easily be generalized for the whole region but should be interpreted as representative of the patterns and flows in the countries covered.

During the reporting period, most of the victims detected in the East Asian countries covered were female. With the exceptions of Japan, the Philippines and Singapore, the East Asian countries did not report adult men among the victims detected. Similarly, the proportion of boys among detected victims in this region was limited in number (less than 5 per cent of total victims) and limited to a few countries. The proportion of males, where detected, among the total number of victims was always less than 10 per cent.

In the Pacific area, Australia reported that 16 adult males were referred to its Support for Trafficked People programme between 2007 and 2010, which accounts for 15 per cent of all detected victims in that country. In South

---

FIG. 39: **Detected victims of trafficking in selected countries in Asia and the Pacific, by age and gender,** late 2000s

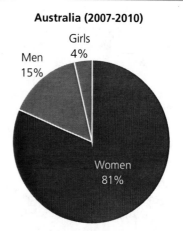

Australia (2007-2010)

Girls 4%
Men 15%
Women 81%

Source: Department of Families, Housing, Community Services and Indigenous Affairs (FaHCSIA).

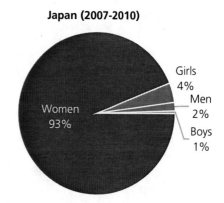

Japan (2007-2010)

Girls 4%
Men 2%
Boys 1%
Women 93%

Source: National Police Agency/Ministry of Justice/ Ministry of Health, Labour and Welfare.

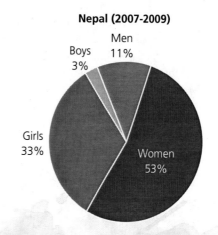

Nepal (2007-2009)

Men 11%
Boys 3%
Girls 33%
Women 53%

Source: Directorate of Women and Children Service Centre.

---

32 The nine countries are Australia, Indonesia, Japan, the Lao People's Democratic Republic, Mongolia, Nepal, the Philippines, Singapore and Thailand.

Asia, Nepal also found that males constituted 15 per cent of detected victims during the same period. Both countries thus registered shares of male trafficking that are in line with the world average.

This region is geographically very diverse, and this is reflected in the age profiles of the victims detected. Australia, Japan and Mongolia reported more adult victims than children; in fact, the presence of minors among the detected victims in those three countries is limited: below 10 per cent. Conversely, countries in South-East Asia consistently reported the proportion of children to be above 15-20 per cent. The information reported by the Lao People's Democratic Republic indicates that most of the victims detected in the country were children. As reported in the *Global Report on Trafficking in Persons* of 2009,[33] the majority of the victims detected in the countries of the Mekong river basin were children. In South Asia, Nepal reported the proportion of victims who were children was about 50 per cent.

2. Traffickers in South Asia, East Asia and the Pacific

Only three countries in South and East Asia and the Pacific provided data regarding the gender of persons prosecuted, and four countries provided data on the persons convicted of trafficking in persons. These data — although limited — further support the observed global pattern of a higher rate of female involvement in trafficking in persons than in other crimes. In addition, with the exception of Japan, the countries report that the participation of women in this crime is equal to or higher than the rate of participation by men.

The general proportion of women among crime convictions in these countries is higher than in Africa and the Americas and is similar to the levels found in Europe. Women account for about 10-25 per cent of convictions for all crimes, and the presence of female human traffickers is more common than in other regions.

The scarcity of information regarding the profile of the offenders in this region is even more acute with regard to the nationality of the offenders. In East Asia, only Japan and Singapore provided information on this aspect of human trafficking. Japan reported that some 23 per cent of persons convicted of trafficking in persons during the reporting period were foreign nationals, while just 7 per

..

33 *Global Report on Trafficking in Persons* (2009), p. 55.

FIG. 40: **Gender of persons convicted of trafficking in persons, selected countries in South and East Asia and the Pacific, 2007-2010**

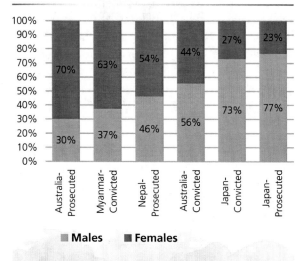

Source: UNODC elaboration of national data.

FIG. 41: **Gender of persons convicted for all crimes, selected countries in South and East Asia and the Pacific, 2006-2009**

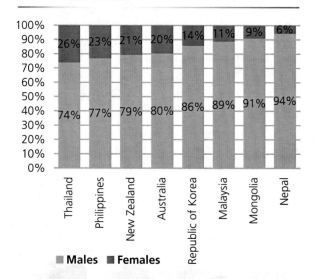

Source: UNODC, United Nations Survey of Crime Trends and Operations of Criminal Justice Systems.

cent of those convicted for all crimes between 2006 and 2009 were foreign nationals. Singapore indicated that the majority of the human trafficking offenders were foreign nationals. Conversely, Australia reported that only local nationals were convicted of human trafficking (although the convicts were reported to be foreign-born). However, there are few criminal proceedings reported by the authorities of Australia.

3. Forms of exploitation in South Asia, East Asia and the Pacific

Only 10 countries[34] in this vast region reported information on the form of exploitation of about 3,000 victims detected between 2007 and 2010. Information was also available concerning the forms of exploitation recorded in Taiwan Province of China. As a consequence, it is difficult to draw firm conclusions regarding the exploitation patterns of trafficking in Asia.

Between 2007 and 2010, trafficking in persons for sexual exploitation and for forced labour were reported to be of almost equal proportions in the countries covered in the region.

FIG. 42:   **Distribution of forms of exploitation detected in South and East Asia and the Pacific, 2007-2010**

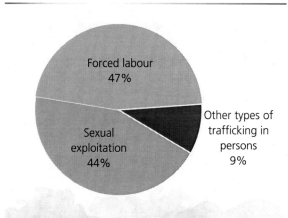

Source: UNODC elaboration of national data.

Trafficking in persons for forced labour, slavery or servitude was the most frequent form of trafficking reported in Indonesia and Taiwan Province of China. In particular, women trafficked for domestic servitude accounted for about 60 per cent of the victims assisted by the International Organization for Migration in Indonesia between 2008 and 2010. Similarly, during those years a large share of the victims assisted in Taiwan Province of China were women exploited in domestic servitude and who had been trafficked from Indonesia, the Philippines, Viet Nam and

34   The 10 countries are Australia, Cambodia, Indonesia, Japan, the Lao People's Democratic Republic, Mongolia, Nepal, the Philippines, Singapore and Thailand.

Bangladesh. In both cases, during the reporting period, women were also trafficked for sexual exploitation. In Australia, authorities are increasingly detecting men and women who have been trafficked into industry sectors other than the sexual exploitation.

In Thailand, trafficking for forced labour accounted for more than 25 per cent of the victims detected in 2011, while 73 per cent of the victims were trafficked for sexual exploitation. The United Nations Inter-Agency Project on Human Trafficking (UNIAP) reported on trafficking victims from the Lao People's Democratic Republic exploited in domestic services, agriculture, fisheries, garment factories and the entertainment sector in 2009. The trafficking of women for exploitation in the category known as the "entertainment sector" has also been reported by the authorities of Japan, and may be a mixed type of exploitation for labour and sexual purposes. UNIAP also reported that sexual exploitation was the major form of exploitation of Cambodian victims trafficked internally or abroad, while a limited number of cases of forced labour was also documented. The Philippines reported that a large number of the victims detected during the period considered were trafficked for sexual exploitation, prostitution and pornography. To a lesser extent, detected victims were also reported to be exploited in forced labour, slavery and child labour. A large part of the Filipinos trafficked within or outside the country were reported to be under debt bondage.

In the other parts of the region here considered, Mongolia and Nepal reported trafficking for sexual exploitation as the most frequent form of trafficking, although trafficking for forced labour or other forms of trafficking were also relatively frequent in these two countries. In detail, 30 per cent of the victims assisted by the Mongolian Gender Equality Centre between 2003 and 2009 were trafficked for forced labour, and 45 per cent for sexual exploitation. The other victims assisted were exploited through other forms of exploitation or for illegal adoption. In Nepal, cases of trafficking for organ removal were also reported by the authorities during the period in question.

4. Trafficking flows in South Asia, East Asia and the Pacific

Trafficking in the subregion of East Asia and the Pacific can be analysed in terms of origin and destination of local, intraregional and long-distance trafficking.

Victims from this subregion are largely trafficked within Asia. From the point of view of the receiving countries, during the reporting period 99 per cent of the victims detected in East Asia and the Pacific were East Asian nationals trafficked across the border or domestically.

Countries and territories of destination in this region include Australia, Japan, Taiwan Province of China and Thailand. Indonesia also reported victims trafficked from other countries, as well as a significant share of domestic trafficking. Domestic trafficking was also reported in Japan and the Philippines, as well as in China, Myanmar and other countries.

A very prominent trafficking flow within East Asia and the Pacific originates from South-East Asia, with the whole East Asia and the Pacific subregion as destination, although victims from China and the Republic of Korea have also been detected. In addition, the countries in the Mekong river basin are characterized by internal trafficking as well as cross-border trafficking into neighbouring countries.

The same pattern described for other regions of the world is also valid for East Asia and the Pacific: victims from relatively poorer countries of the subregion are trafficked to comparatively richer countries. Authorities in Thailand

detected victims from Cambodia, the Lao People's Democratic Republic and Myanmar, while at the same time, Thai victims have been detected in Australia, China and Japan. Japan reported to have detected victims from China, Indonesia, the Philippines and the Republic of Korea. Australia also reported victims trafficked from Malaysia and the Republic of Korea.

Thus, a large part of the trafficking in East Asia and the Pacific is intraregional and most countries of the subregion play a role as both origin and destination countries. The only exceptions to this pattern are Australia and Japan, which receive only cross-border trafficking (i.e. they are not origin for cross-border trafficking).

Although the share is small (less than 1 per cent) compared with the total number of victims detected in the subregion, East Asia and the Pacific is also a destination for victims trafficked from other regions. Victims from Eastern Europe and Central Asia were detected or repatriated from South-East Asian countries between 2007 and 2010. South American victims were detected or repatriated from five countries of this region during the same period.

As for the origin of long-distance trafficking flows, the prominence of East Asian trafficking to the rest of the world was already documented in the *Global Report on*

MAP 18: **Proportion of trafficked East Asians among the total number of victims detected at specific destinations, 2007-2010**

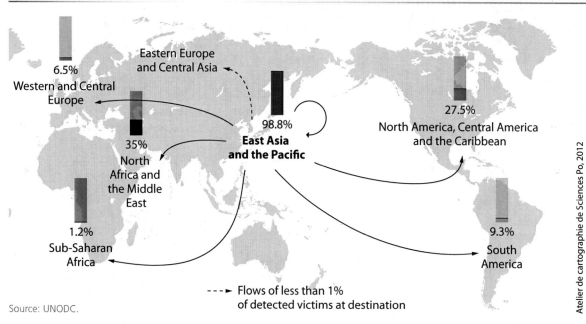

Source: UNODC.

Atelier de cartographie de Sciences Po, 2012

Trafficking 2009.[35] Between 2007 and 2010, victims from East Asia were detected in 64 countries around the world, including in sub-Saharan Africa, the Middle East, Central and South America and Eastern Europe. During the reporting period, East Asian victims accounted for about 7 per cent of the victims detected in Western and Central Europe, 22 per cent of victims detected in the Americas, and 35 per cent of victims detected in North Africa and the Middle East. No specific country can be identified as the main origin of the East Asian long-distance trafficking flow. Victims of different nationalities, including Chinese, Filipino, Thai, Vietnamese and others, were detected in or repatriated from various countries in other regions outside Asia between 2007 and 2010.

Although the diffusion of the trafficking flows originating in South Asia is more limited, it should not be underestimated. The region is also an origin of long-distance trafficking flows. Indications of the wide diffusion of South Asian trafficking were reported from all the subregions considered in this report. During the reporting period, victims from South Asia have been detected in or repatriated from Southern Africa, South America and 13 European countries. In the Middle East, South Asians victims account for about 23 per cent of the detected victims.

Victims originating in Bangladesh were detected in the United Arab Emirates, and Nepalese and Sri Lankan victims were detected in Israel. Lebanon also detected victims of those nationalities. Indian and Pakistani victims were detected in Western and Central Europe. South Asians were also detected in the United States. Thus, there is a global dimension to the flows originating in South Asia.

Core results: patterns and flows in South Asia, East Asia and the Pacific

* The majority of the victims detected in the countries of South and East Asia and the Pacific in the reporting period were female (women and girls).

* The proportion of individuals convicted of trafficking in persons in this region who were women is higher than the proportion of women convicted of other crimes. It is also higher than the proportion of female convictions reported in other regions.

* During the reporting period, 47 per cent of the victims detected in the countries of South and East Asia and the Pacific reporting for this study were trafficked for forced labour, while 44 per cent were trafficked for sexual exploitation. Exploitation in domestic servitude was frequently reported.

MAP 19: **Proportion of trafficked South Asians among total victims detected at specific destinations,** 2007-2010

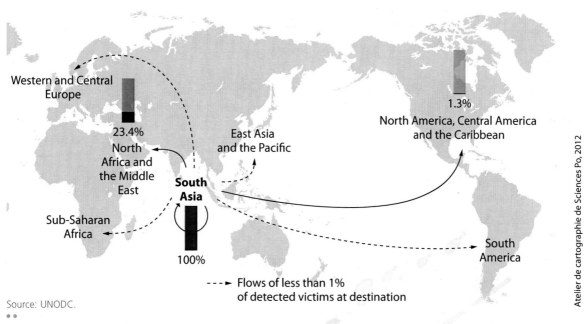

Source: UNODC.

●●

35 *Global Report on Trafficking in Persons* (2009), p. 61.

* Most of the trafficking flows relevant to the South Asian, East Asian and Pacific countries covered in this report are intraregional (i.e. flows within the region). In the reporting period, most of the victims detected here were either trafficked within the region or within the country of origin.

* In the period considered by this report, East Asia was confirmed as a significant source region victims of trafficking in persons at the global level. East Asian victims were detected in 64 countries around the world in all regions and subregions considered in this report, often in significant numbers.

* South Asian victims were detected in a wide range of destinations in different regions of the world.

D. AFRICA AND THE MIDDLE EAST

Information from 36 countries in Africa and the Middle East was considered for the preparation of this report. Of these, 12 countries belong to the subregion of North Africa and the Middle East and 24 countries belong to the subregion of sub-Saharan Africa. Countries did not necessarily provide information for all indicators. The data coverage for this region is relatively weak.

1. Victims of trafficking in Africa and the Middle East

Information on the profile of the victims detected during the reporting period was provided by 14 countries in Africa and the Middle East. Profiles were available for about 6,300 victims of trafficking in persons reported in the region between 2007 and 2010 (or more recently). More than 4,200 of those victims were children (68 per cent).

FIG. 43: **Victims of trafficking in Africa and the Middle East, by age profile, 2007-2010**

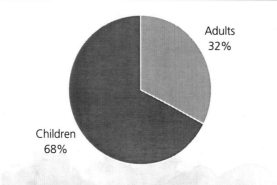

Source: UNODC elaboration of national data.

The profile of the victims reported by some countries in sub-Saharan Africa may have been affected by the current legislation on trafficking in persons. At the time of preparation of this report, Côte d'Ivoire and Togo had legislation which criminalized only child trafficking, while Burkina Faso, Mali and Uganda had only recently included adult trafficking in their criminal codes. As a consequence, most or all of the victims detected by these countries during the reporting period were children.

When considering countries with long-standing and comprehensive legislation on trafficking in persons, however, the proportion of child trafficking in this region was still larger than the global average. In Nigeria, for example, children accounted for about half of the victims of trafficking detected during the reporting period. Ghana and Sierra Leone reported that a vast majority of the victims detected were children.

As the available official data are relatively limited and tend to be affected by the national legal contexts, it may be useful to consider additional information from other sources. Reports by other intergovernmental organizations have confirmed the notion that human trafficking in sub-Saharan Africa is characterized by a significant presence of child victims. In 2009, the United Nations Operation in Côte d'Ivoire reported only child trafficking cases. Those cases involved children aged 8 to 16 from countries neighbouring Côte d'Ivoire who had been trafficked for child labour and sexual exploitation. In the same country, the International Organization for Migration reported having assisted 70 victims of trafficking in persons between 2006 and 2008, 66 of them children. Similarly, in 2009, the former United Nations Mission in the Central African Republic and Chad reported grave concerns regarding the disappearance from refugee camps of children who were subsequently used in the armed forces operating in Chad. In the same period, the United Nations Organization Stabilization Mission in the Democratic Republic of the Congo (MONUSCO) reported that children were trafficked to become child soldiers as well as for forced marriages or forced labour. Although the data available might have possible biases, it seems that child trafficking is the major form of trafficking in at least some parts of the African continent.

The pattern in Southern Africa may be different. According to a regional study commissioned by the Government of South Africa,[36] in the past few years, adult women were

· ·

36 National Prosecuting Authority of South Africa, *Tsireledzani: Under-*

FIG. 44: **Share of child victims among total trafficking victims detected in Nigeria,** January 2008-March 2010

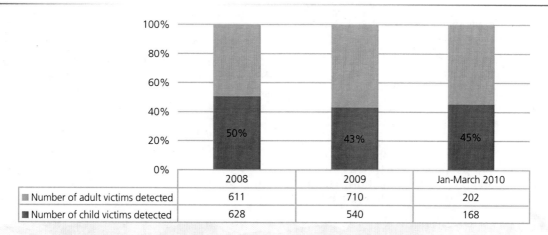

	2008	2009	Jan-March 2010
Number of adult victims detected	611	710	202
Number of child victims detected	628	540	168

Source: National Agency for the Prohibition of Traffic in Persons and Other Related Matters.

more frequently trafficked for sexual exploitation, although children were also reported to have been trafficked. In 2010, a study on the situation in Lesotho raised concerns about the prevalence of adult men trafficked for forced labour in the mining sector.[37]

Available official data indicate that adult trafficking was more prevalent than child trafficking in the Middle East. While the United Arab Emirates detected more adult women than other victims, Qatar detected more adult men than women. The other countries generally registered a relatively low share of child trafficking, although Egypt detected a large share of boys as victims between 2009 and 2010. This should be seen in light of the fact that this country introduced the offence of adult trafficking in May 2010.

2. Traffickers in Africa and the Middle East

A limited number of countries (eight countries) in this region provided information regarding the profile of the offenders. According to these sparse data, Africa and the Middle East is the region with the lowest participation of women in trafficking in persons. About 20 per cent of the people prosecuted and convicted during the reporting period were females.

• •

standing the Dimensions of Human Trafficking in Southern Africa (March 2010).

37 United Nations Development Programme/Ministry of Home Affairs, Public Safety and Parliamentary Affairs of Lesotho, *Rapid Assessment of Trafficking in Persons in Lesotho* (2011).

FIG. 45: **Persons prosecuted and convicted by gender — selected countries in Africa and the Middle East,** 2007-2010

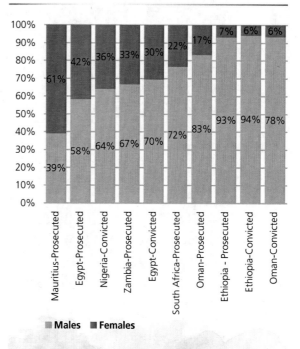

Source: UNODC elaboration of national data.

The relatively small share of female offenders should be seen in the light of the generally low participation of women in all forms of crime in this region (rarely above 10 per cent). In general, female offending is lower in Africa than in other parts of the world.

As far as the nationality of the offenders is concerned, Africa and the Middle East tend to follow the global pattern, with destination countries more likely to report foreign nationals among those prosecuted for or convicted of trafficking in persons. Gulf countries such as Qatar and Oman register a high presence of foreign traffickers. When comparing the share of foreign traffickers to the share of persons convicted for other crimes, however, it becomes clear that trafficking in persons follows the regular criminological pattern of this area.

FIG. 46: **Shares of foreign nationals and own nationals convicted of trafficking and all crimes, selected countries in North Africa and the Middle East,** 2007-2010

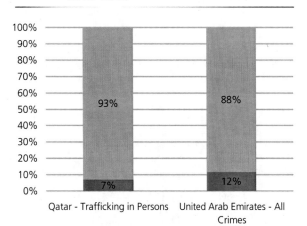

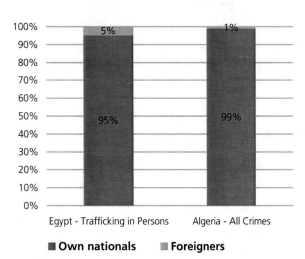

In sub-Saharan Africa (apart from Mauritius, which reported that only local nationals were convicted for trafficking in persons), the number of foreign nationals among the few criminal proceedings conducted during the reporting period was surprisingly high. Ghana, for example, reported that of a total of five convictions, three were of East Asians. Lesotho recorded its first trafficking in persons-related conviction in January 2012, also of an East Asian citizen.

More information is needed to understand what appears to be a disproportionate presence of foreign nationals among the few convictions reported in some sub-Saharan African countries.

3. Forms of exploitation in Africa and the Middle East

The patterns of exploitation reported in Africa and the Middle East are based on information received concerning some 1,100 victims detected between 2007 and 2010. Information was available for 16 countries in the region: six in the Middle East and North Africa, and 10 in sub-Saharan Africa.

During the reporting period, Africa and the Middle East reported an overall higher share of victims trafficked for forced labour compared with other regions. Forced labour is the most frequently detected form of trafficking in the region. Higher percentages of victims trafficked for other purposes were also recorded.

FIG. 47: **Distribution of forms of exploitation detected in Africa and the Middle East,** 2007-2010

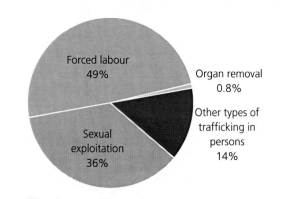

Trafficking for sexual exploitation in this region should not be disregarded, however. During the period considered, the Middle Eastern countries, in particular, reported more cases of trafficking for sexual exploitation than other forms of exploitation. This is the case for Oman and the United Arab Emirates. A study conducted in Egypt also reported cases of trafficking for sexual exploitation in that country, as well as trafficking for forced marriages, child labour and begging.[38] The Syrian Arab Republic also reported cases of trafficking for begging as well as different cases of trafficking for organ removal.

Israel, which for long detected only trafficking for sexual exploitation, reported a predominance of victims for forced labour in 2009, 2010 and 2011. Most of these victims — more than 100 — were Thai men sheltered by the Israeli authorities after having been trafficked for forced labour in the agricultural sector. Trafficking for forced labour was largely detected in countries in sub-Saharan Africa (Ethiopia, Ghana and South Africa). The forms of trafficking ranged from children exploited in the fishing industry in Ghana's Lake Volta, detected by the Ghanaian authorities, as well as by the International Organization for Migration, to women and men working in rural sites of artisanal exploitation of natural resources in the Democratic Republic of the Congo, documented by MONUSCO in the areas surrounding the mining sites in this country. MONUSCO also documented the role of the different armed forces operating in the country in trafficking children, women and men for different types of forced labour, for instance as carriers of ammunition and similar tasks. In Côte d'Ivoire, the United Nations Operation in Côte d'Ivoire reported cases of child trafficking for forced labour involving nationals of Burkina Faso in 2009, and victims of trafficking exploited in domestic servitude in 2007. In South Africa, victims of trafficking have been reported to be exploited largely for domestic servitude, as well as in agriculture. Authorities have also documented cases of trafficking of Togolese children for domestic servitude in Gabon.

The phenomenon of child soldiers, which is relatively frequently reported in sub-Saharan Africa, has also been detected during the present reporting period. The trafficking of children for the purpose of using them as armed combatants was reported in the Democratic Republic of the Congo and Chad by the United Nations operations

38 Egyptian National Center for Social and Criminological Research, *Trafficking in Human Beings in the Egyptian Society: Patterns, Variables and Actors* (2010).

in those countries, and by non-governmental organizations in Burundi, where former child soldiers found assistance. According to information provided by MONUSCO, there have been allegations of systematic door-to-door recruitment of children and young men in areas occupied by irregular armed forces. During years considered in the present report, the former United Nations Mission in the Central African Republic and Chad reported the recruitment of children for use as combatants by different armed forces active in these areas. The recruitment occurred inside the refugee camps sheltering the internally displaced population in this region. The irregular armed forces were also reported to have been responsible for other forms of trafficking such as forced marriages of underage girls and using women as sex slaves.

During the reporting period, trafficking for the removal of organs was detected in various Middle Eastern countries. During the same period, cases of trafficking for the use of body parts in rituals were reported in East and Southern Africa. Though, as for any type of human trafficking in sub-Saharan Africa, little data are available, cases were reported by all countries of a vast area stretching from Lake Victoria to Mozambique and South Africa. The few reports available indicate that vulnerable groups such as women, children and albinos were targeted for practices connected to "muti" (local traditional medicine) or other rituals (see textbox on page 39).

4. Trafficking flows in Africa and the Middle East

For the purpose of this report, information regarding the nationality of the victims detected between 2007 and 2010 was reported for more than 1,600 victims by 18 countries in Africa and the Middle East.

About 500 of these victims were detected in the Middle East, which is a prominent destination region for victims trafficked from other regions. More than 300 of these victims were trafficked from other continents, in particular from East Asia and South Asia.

Among the East Asians victims, citizens of Thailand were detected in Bahrain and Israel. Nationals of Indonesia and the Philippines were also detected in the subregion. South Asian victims detected in the Middle East during the reporting period included nationals of Bangladesh, Nepal and Sri Lanka.

Countries in the Middle East also reported having detected a significant number of trafficking victims from Ethiopia

MAP 20: **Origin of victims trafficked to the Middle East, as a proportion of the total number of victims detected, 2007-2010**

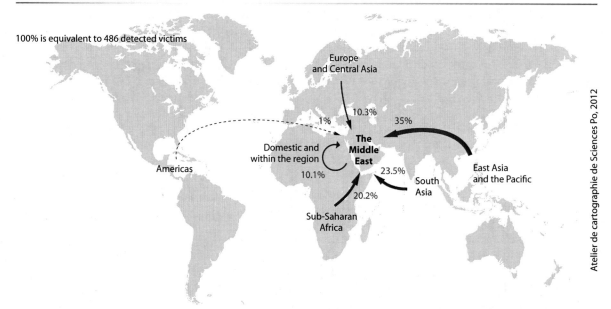

100% is equivalent to 486 detected victims

Europe
and Central Asia

10.3%

1%

35%

The
Middle
East

Domestic and
within the region

10.1%

East Asia
and the Pacific

Americas

23.5%

South
Asia

20.2%

Sub-Saharan
Africa

Atelier de cartographie de Sciences Po, 2012

Source: UNODC.

and Eritrea, as well as nationals of Iraqis and other countries of the Middle East. Internal trafficking in the Middle East is significantly lower than in other regions.

Victims that had been trafficked in sub-Saharan Africa were mainly nationals of the same subregion or the same geographical area. West African countries reported that West African victims are trafficked within the same country or into neighbouring countries, with the exceptions of Filipino victims detected in Côte d'Ivoire and limited episodes of trafficking of Chinese victims in Ghana. The same conclusions can be drawn from the limited information available in East African countries, where the few cases of trafficking reported involved East African victims. Reports from Southern Africa were also limited, although for this area it is possible to identify some victims originating in other continents. For example, Thai victims were detected in South Africa, and the first conviction for human trafficking registered in Lesotho concerned a Chinese national exploiting a Chinese victim in 2011.

Outside Africa, African victims were mainly detected in Western and Central Europe, where about 3,000 African trafficking victims were identified in 22 countries between 2007 and 2010. These trafficking flows concerned relatively few nationalities — mainly West Africans, who account for the vast majority of the African victims detected here (2,300 victims). Nigerian victims were

detected in 16 countries in Western and Central Europe, where they account for 11 per cent of all victims detected. Citizens of Cameroon, Ghana, Guinea and Sierra Leone have also been identified as victims of trafficking in many European countries.

As for trafficking originating from other African countries, Ugandan victims were detected in the United Kingdom and other European countries. Other East African victims (from Ethiopia, Eritrea and Somalia) were detected in Scandinavian countries.

With respect to victims from North Africa, Moroccan victims were detected in nine countries in West and Central Europe, including Belgium, France, Italy, the Netherlands and Spain. Algerian victims were trafficked in France and Norway.

As reported above, trafficking of African victims also took place in countries of the Middle East. East Africans (Eritreans and Ethiopians) and North Africans were detected in the Middle East between 2007 and 2010.

Trafficking originating in Southern Africa is mainly limited to countries within the subregion. Sporadic cases of Southern African nationals who were victims of human trafficking in other regions were reported. Episodes of trafficking involving Southern African victims were detected in Europe.

MAP 21: **Proportion of trafficked West Africans among all victims detected at specific destinations, 2007-2010**

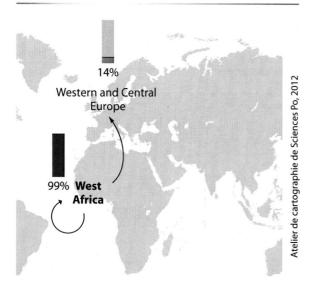

Source: UNODC.

MAP 23: **Proportion of trafficked North Africans among all victims detected at specific destinations, 2007-2010**

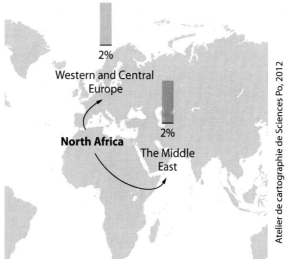

Source: UNODC.

MAP 22: **Proportion of trafficked East Africans among all victims detected at specific destinations, 2007-2010**

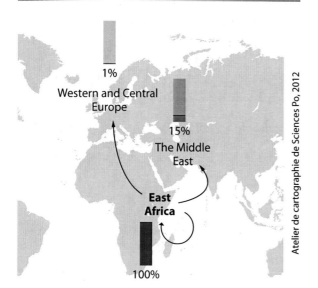

Source: UNODC.

Core results: patterns and flows in Africa and the Middle East

- The majority (67 per cent) of the victims of trafficking detected in the region during the reporting period were children.

- During the reporting period, 49 per cent of the victims detected in Africa and the Middle East were trafficked for forced labour and 36 per cent for sexual exploitation.

- Victims of other forms of exploitation, including child soldiers and trafficking for rituals, accounted for 14 per cent of cases. Cases of trafficking for organ removal were reported in the Middle East.

- During the years considered by this report, the Middle East was mainly an area of destination for victims trafficked from East Asia and South Asia. East Africans, Eastern Europeans and Central Asians were also detected in the Middle East.

- A large proportion of the victims detected in sub-Saharan Africa are trafficked within the country of origin or within the subregion. Trafficking of victims from West Africa accounts for a significant share of trafficking in Europe. East Africans account for an important share of the victims in the Middle East and were also detected in Western and Central Europe.

The way forward for research on trafficking in persons at the national, regional and international levels

The *Global Report on Trafficking in Persons* of 2009 advocated for more and better information on trafficking in persons to be collected at the national level in order to facilitate improved analysis at the international level. That report highlighted the knowledge crisis with respect to human trafficking that continued to exist 10 years after the Trafficking in Persons Protocol was opened for signature.

The conclusion to the analytical section of the present *Global Report on Trafficking in Persons 2012* can only reiterate that message. There is now clearly more information available from national authorities. Better data are collected and published today than just three years ago, which means that improvements have been made in terms of information-sharing and transparency. At the same time, there is still a large knowledge gap about trafficking in persons in vast areas of the world.

Solving the persistent knowledge crisis with regard to trafficking in persons requires significant progress related to two major challenges: first, the still relatively weak criminal justice response to this crime continues to limit the explanatory power of reports emerging from law enforcement sources. Secondly, the absence of a standardized and widely accepted methodology hampers estimations of the real number of victims (detected and undetected).

As far as the first challenge is concerned, the problem is the difficulty of extrapolating patterns and flows emerging from official statistics. The rich information available for Europe has made it possible to provide solid, meaningful analyses on the dynamics of trafficking in persons in that region. It is possible, for instance, to assess whether certain trafficking flows are decreasing or increasing.

Making better data available in a standardized form and with regular periodic frequency would lead to better analysis, even if the data had all the familiar limitations of criminal justice statistics. Accessing those data for trafficking in persons at the global level would make it possible to test hypotheses such as the possibility of supply displacements when certain flows decrease, or similar analyses.

This could ultimately lead to the provision of statistically reliable predictions on trends, patterns and flows, which could, in turn, be used to develop better polices to prevent and combat trafficking in persons.

At the same time, this report shows that regions have different capacities to detect and report victims of trafficking in persons. While European countries are relatively effective in this task, not enough victims are detected in developing countries to rely exclusively on the patterns and flows emerging from the detected cases in order to have an accurate picture of what is actually happening in those countries.

These considerations lead to the second challenge, which is the current absence of tools to observe the dark figure of the crime of trafficking in persons at the international level. Although some promising pilot research methods have been implemented at the local level, there is still no broadly accepted methodological approach to assess the trafficking in persons globally, beyond the analysis of cases officially detected by local authorities.

The complex variety of the trafficking flows, the diversity of the forms of exploitation, which are sometimes not even codified or clearly defined, and — even more — the prominence of domestic trafficking in dispersed areas of the world show that assessing the size of human trafficking in terms of the number of victims is not an easy task. There is a real need for field research in order to estimate the number of victims trafficked in specific trafficking flows or in specific forms of trafficking.

The mandate of the biennial *Global Report on Trafficking in Persons* opens the door to a long-term strategy to test and implement proper methodologies to better assess patterns and flows of human trafficking also in those areas where the criminal justice response is weak.

There are no easy shortcuts for such a difficult target. The implementation of this strategy will clearly require a coordinated global research effort.

CHAPTER III
GLOBAL RESPONSES:
COMMITMENT TO COMBATING
TRAFFICKING IN PERSONS

The commitment of Member States to combat trafficking in persons, especially women and children, was noted from the onset of the negotiation process of the United Nations Convention against Transnational Organized Crime and its additional Protocols. The Protocol to Prevent, Suppress and Punish Trafficking in Persons, especially Women and Children received the required 40 ratifications by 2003, enabling it to enter into force in record time.[39] This reflected the broad consensus that countries must act in concert to address trafficking in persons. The sense of global commitment continued to manifest itself over the years through the steadily growing number of ratifications. At the time of writing,[40] 152 United Nations Member States had ratified the Trafficking in Persons Protocol.

The growing number of ratifications of the Trafficking in Persons Protocol has been met by a growing number of countries passing legislation covering all or most forms[41] of trafficking in persons. Even though 12 years after the adoption of the Protocol,[42] the national legislative framework is still not comprehensive it covers human trafficking crimes fully or at least partially in most countries of the world. Regional instruments following the model of the Trafficking in Persons Protocol have been created and plans of action for the implementation of the Protocol have been established in several countries.

There are also many other successes in the action against human trafficking. Global awareness on trafficking has increased significantly and several Member States have shown real initiative to combat this crime. However, conviction rates in many countries are still embarrassingly low, prevention efforts fail to reach their targets and the protection of the vulnerable ones is a far cry from the objectives presented in the Protocol. There are many reasons for the lack of implementation of the Protocol during these ten years. Particularly, three challenges are discussed in this chapter; the lack of knowledge on human traffick-

TABLE 2: **Matrix of the elements of the trafficking in persons offence**

ACT	MEANS		PURPOSE	
Recruitment	Threat or use of force		Exploitation of the prostitution of others	
Transportation	Other forms of coercion		Sexual exploitation	
Transfer	Abduction		Labour exploitation	
Harbouring	Fraud		Slavery or other slavery-like situations	
Receipt of persons	Deception	+	Organ removal	= TRAFFICKING IN PERSONS
	Abuse of power		Et cetera	
	Abuse of a position of vulnerability			
	Giving or receiving of payments or benefits to achieve the consent of a person having control over another person			

39 Inter-Agency Coordination Group against Trafficking in Persons (ICAT), *An analytical review - 10 years on from the adoption of the United Nations Trafficking in Persons Protocol,* October 2010, p.36.

40 30 August 2012.

41 Most forms of trafficking in persons means at a minimum trafficking in persons for sexual exploitation and trafficking in persons for forced labour, without a restriction regarding gender or age.

42 General Assembly resolution A/RES/55/25, *United Nations Convention against Transnational Organized Crime,* 15 November 2000.

ing, the lack of capacity to address it and the lack of evaluation to assess the impact of action.

Following the mandate of the Global Plan of Action, this chapter focuses on the criminalization of trafficking in persons as defined in the Trafficking in Persons Protocol in order to study the legislative and criminal justice response progress. The definition of trafficking in persons is composed of three elements: the act, the means and the purpose. Using a combination of these three constituent elements, the Trafficking in Persons Protocol defines the crime of trafficking in persons as outlined in the matrix in table 2.

Trafficking in persons is not just about transportation, it is not only about exploitation, or about being duped. Trafficking in persons is often a complicated process which includes all these phases. Law enforcement and the criminal justice system as a whole need to be aware of the exact criminal act defined as trafficking in persons in order to identify cases properly. This facilitates investigations which look beyond the exploiter to ensure that all those involved along the process, sometimes in many different countries, are targeted. Through international cooperation, police and the criminal justice system need to work across borders, which are so easily crossed by criminals, to ensure that traffickers are investigated, prosecuted and convicted. Any criminal justice response to trafficking in persons needs to have a victim-centred approach to ensure that victims of trafficking in persons are properly identified at all stages of the trafficking process, that their needs are met and that they are equipped to participate in the criminal proceedings should they wish to do so.

Before exploring in detail the challenges involved in implementing the Trafficking in Persons Protocol, first, a look at the current implementation situation through two indicators of the criminal justice response: the compliance of legislation with the Trafficking in Persons Protocol's definition and convictions for trafficking in persons crimes around the world. Naturally, it should be kept in mind that criminal justice requirements form only one part of the commitments laid down in the Protocol.

A. STATUS OF IMPLEMENTATION OF THE TRAFFICKING IN PERSONS PROTOCOL – FOCUS ON CRIMINALIZATION

This first edition of the Global Report on Trafficking in

Persons, as mandated by the Global Plan of Action, allows for clear conclusions to be drawn on legislative and criminal justice response progress, with a focus on the criminalization of trafficking in persons as defined in the Trafficking in Persons Protocol. In the years to come, the collection of data will be broadened to cover more elements of trafficking in persons patterns and processes.

1. Legislation

Progress made at the global level

Before the adoption of the Trafficking in Persons Protocol more than ten years ago, several countries did not have any legislation addressing trafficking in persons, or if they did, it mainly covered women and/or children who were trafficked for sexual exploitation. The situation has changed dramatically over the last ten years.

The 2009 *Global Report on Trafficking in Persons*[43] showed the positive impact of the entry into force of the Trafficking in Persons Protocol with the number of countries having legislation criminalizing all or most forms of trafficking in persons doubling between 2003 and 2008 among the 155 countries and territories concerned. The positive trend has continued over the last three years.

Member States have continued to pass legislation or amending it in order to comply with the Trafficking in

FIG. 48: **Criminalization of trafficking in persons with a specific offence (for 162 countries and territories),** as of November 2008 and August 2012

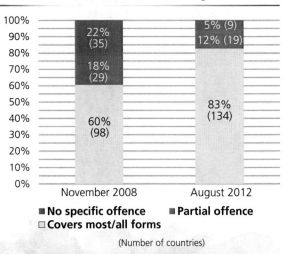

(Number of countries)

Source: UNODC elaboration on national data.

43 UNODC-UN.GIFT, *Global Report on Trafficking in Persons*, 2009.

Persons Protocol, as shown in figure 48. In this case, the number of countries and territories assessed with regard to their anti-trafficking legislation was broadened to a sample of 162.

In November 2008, about 80 per cent of the 162 countries and territories had a specific offence in their domestic legislation, covering all or some forms of trafficking in persons. A little more than 20 per cent of countries did not have a specific trafficking in persons offence.

In 2012, the percentage of countries without a specific offence has more than halved, with only 9 countries or territories out of 162 not having a specific offence in their domestic legislation. More than 90 per cent of the 162 countries and territories covered by the present report have specific legislation covering fully or partially all or most forms of trafficking in persons. This means that at least 134 countries and territories in the world have criminalized trafficking and established a strong legislative basis for cooperation, exchange of good practices and a common understanding of what trafficking in persons is and that victims of this crime are to be protected. An additional 19 countries have legislation covering trafficking in persons partially, either by focusing on women or children only, or by covering one type of exploitation only, such as sexual exploitation. Progress can also be noted on that front; the percentage of countries criminalizing only some aspects of trafficking in persons decreased from 17 per cent in 2008 to 11 per cent in 2012, as countries amended their legislation in accordance with the Trafficking in Persons Protocol.

Progress made at the regional level

Of the nine countries covered by this report that do not have an offence on trafficking in persons in domestic law (compared to 35 in 2008), African and Small Island States are the two groups that emerge most prominently.

When looking at countries with no legislation or legislation with partial criminalization (28 countries in total), African States account for 60 per cent of this group, as shown in figure 49. The partiality of legislation in Asia and South America should also be noted, since it may have an impact on a large population in these regions.

Despite the remaining lack of a specific offence covering most or all forms of trafficking in persons in several African countries, progress has been made in that region as well. There has been an increase in the number of sub-Saharan African countries that have legislation covering

FIG. 49: **Number of countries with no or partial legislation in August 2012**

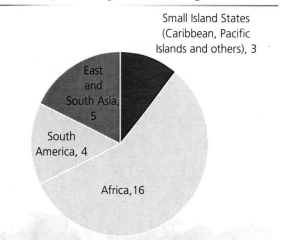

Source: UNODC elaboration on national data.

all or most forms of trafficking in persons. The number of countries that include trafficking in persons in their domestic legislation increased from 12 in 2008 to 23 in 2012. In addition, the number of countries without an offence significantly decreased. In North Africa and the Middle East, several countries introduced comprehensive legislation during the period considered. While in November 2008 just four countries criminalized most or all forms of trafficking, in August 2012, this number had increased to 10. The number of countries in Africa and the Middle

FIG. 50: **Percentage of countries with full, partial or no legislation on trafficking in persons in Africa and the Middle East,** November 2008 and August 2012

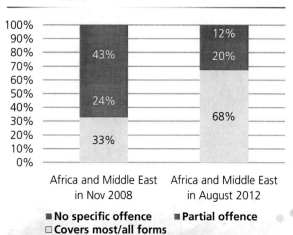

Source: UNODC elaboration on national data.

FIG. 51: **Percentage of countries with full, partial or no legislation on trafficking in persons in the regions considered for this Report,** November 2008 and August 2012

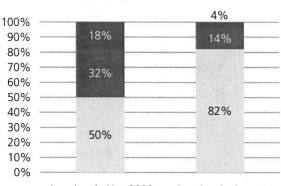

Americas in Nov 2008 — Americas in August 2012

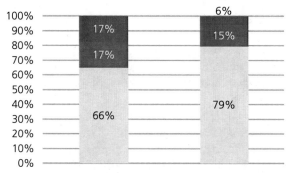

South Asia, East Asia and the Pacific in Nov 2008 — South Asia, East Asia and the Pacific in August 2012

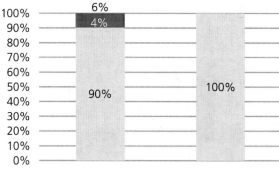

Europe and Central Asia in Nov 2008 — Europe and Central Asia in August 2012

■ **No specific offence**
■ **Partial offence**
□ **Covers most/all forms**

Source: UNODC elaboration on national data.

East with a specific offence on trafficking in persons in line with the Trafficking in Persons Protocol more than doubled in the last three years.

Similar trends can be found in all other regions. The number of countries (covered by this Report) with legislation covering all or most forms of trafficking in persons is increasing, while the number of countries without an offence is decreasing.

Summing up, the positive impact of the Trafficking in Persons Protocol continues as the trend starting in 2003 shows. In most countries, the legislation currently covers most or all forms of trafficking and there are only nine countries without a specific offence of trafficking in persons in their domestic legislation. Member States continue to work towards meeting their obligations to criminalize trafficking in Persons under the Protocol. Efforts must not diminish and these encouraging results need to be sustained until there is universal ratification of the Trafficking in Persons Protocol followed by universal criminalization of all forms of trafficking in persons.

In continuation of the dispositions included in the Trafficking in Persons Protocol, the United Nations Global Plan of Action to Combat Trafficking in Persons adopted in July 2010 showed the strong and continued commitment of Member States to taking measures to implement all national legal instruments that criminalize trafficking in persons.[44]

Tools such as the UNODC Model Law against Trafficking in Persons are key to supporting country-level efforts to develop or amend their national legislation. In addition, Member States should use the available technical assistance tools to strengthen their capacity to criminalize trafficking in persons.

2. Criminal justice response – convictions

The analysis of some elements of the criminal justice response to trafficking in persons in this report is based on information and data received from 132 countries. Depending on the element of the criminal justice response under consideration, the number of countries covered changes. This is clearly indicated so that there is no misrepresentation of the results.

44 Op. 43 of the United Nations Global Plan of Action to Combat Trafficking in Persons.

The UNODC Model Law against Trafficking in Persons

The UNODC Model Law against Trafficking in Persons assists States in implementing the provisions contained in the Trafficking in Persons Protocol. It aims to facilitate the review and amendment of existing legislation as well as the adoption of new laws. The Model Law covers not only the criminalization of trafficking in persons and related offences, but also the different aspects of assistance to victims as well as establishing cooperation between different state authorities and NGOs. Each provision is accompanied by a detailed commentary, legal sources and examples, providing several options for legislators, as appropriate. It provides sources and examples for the interpretation of key concepts of the Trafficking in Persons Protocol, and ensures that other relevant instruments are taken into consideration when implementing the Protocol. The Model Law addresses: basic criminal offences; provisions specific to trafficking in persons; ancillary offences and offences related to trafficking in persons; victims and witness protection; assistance and compensation; immigration and return; prevention, training and cooperation and regulatory power.

The time period covered by the report is 2007-2010.[45] The cumulative absolute number of convictions for trafficking in persons is between 5,500 and 7,000 per year for the 132 countries covered. There are slight differences depending on the specific year considered within the period. In addition, some countries also reported convictions only for some years and not for the entire period.[46]

A trend analysis on the absolute numbers of convictions shows an overall increase. This may suggest an overall increase in the criminal justice response to trafficking in persons, but of course this depends on the level of representativeness of the sample considered. Among the 132 countries covered in this Report, 84 reported on their convictions for more than two consecutive years. Among them there were more countries reporting increases than decreases in the number of convictions between 2007 and 2010, as shown in figure 52.

The number of convictions is still very low, however. Among the 132 countries included in this report, 16 per cent did not record a single conviction between 2007 and 2010. Although there has been an improvement compared to the 2009 Global Report, in which two out of five countries had not recorded a single conviction, it can still be concluded that significant impunity remains with regard to trafficking in persons offences.

Some 23 per cent of the countries recorded a very low number of convictions; between 1 and 10 convictions per

FIG. 52: **Trends in the number of recorded convictions between 2007 and 2010,** percentage of countries

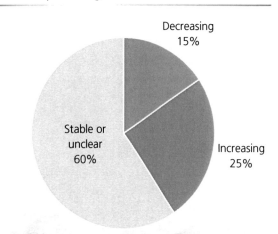

Source: UNODC elaboration on national data.

year between 2007 and 2010. Another 25 per cent of the countries recorded between 10 and 50 convictions in at least one year between 2007 and 2010. For one in five countries, information on the number of convictions was not available for any of the years considered. This lack of information again highlights the need for stronger data collection and information sharing methods.

From a regional perspective, Africa and the Middle East is the region where less convictions were recorded. About 40 per cent of the 36 countries of that region considered in this Report did not record a single conviction during the reporting period. The share increases to about 60 per cent if the minimum number of convictions per year is set at 10.

---

45 The period may change depending on the available data: for example, the information on legislation covers 2008-2012 while the criminal justice response data cover 2007-2010.

46 The analysis conducted in this section relies solely on the comparison of the number of convictions. The nature of the data does not allow for a qualitative analysis of the reported convictions.

FIG. 53: **Number of convictions recorded per year, percentage of countries, 2007-2010**

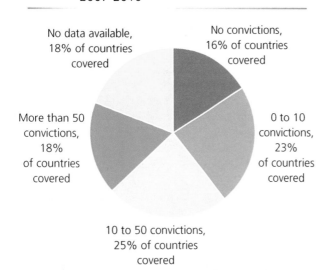

Source: UNODC elaboration on national data.

Asia and Europe appear to have better results as far as convictions for trafficking in persons is concerned. The area of complete impunity, where no convictions have been recorded, is about 5 per cent in South and East Asia and the Pacific, and 2 per cent in Europe and Central Asia.

FIG. 54: **Number of convictions recorded per year, percentage of countries, by region, 2007-2010**

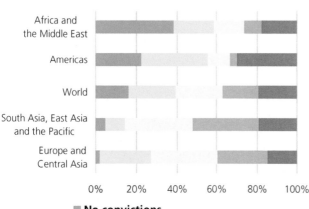

■ **No convictions**
■ **Between 0 and 10 convictions per year**
Between 10 and 50 convictions
■ **More than 50 convictions**
■ **No data available**

Source: UNODC elaboration on national data.

However, it is important to note that Asian countries are in general larger and more populous than European ones. Therefore, it is necessary to review conviction rates, that is, the number of persons convicted per 100,000 persons, to gain a clear understanding of the successful criminal justice response to trafficking in persons worldwide.

Conviction rates

The proper way to present a comparative analysis of the status of the criminal justice response among countries should be on the basis of the standardization of the variable according to the number of people in the country. However, the number of convictions for trafficking in persons globally is so low that presenting the figures in absolute terms as is done in the previous section is the best way to give a clear picture of the extent to which traffickers enjoy impunity around the world.

Nevertheless, undertaking an analysis of the conviction rates does not provide a more positive picture of the situation. Among the 100 countries which provided information on the number of convictions for trafficking in persons for the year 2010 (excluding a limited number of exceptions), the rate ranged between 0 and 1.6 per 100,000 inhabitants. As a matter of fact, if the distribution of countries is considered according to the conviction rates (see figure 55) the majority of the countries registered conviction rates between 0 and 0.6. A conviction rate above 1 was registered in very few cases, and the rate rose above 1.6 per 100,000 persons in only two cases. The mean value for the conviction rates in 2010 among these 100 countries is 0.154 per 100,000 people.

An indicative comparison with other types of crime reinforces the fact that the conviction rate for trafficking in persons is extremely low. The conviction rate for trafficking in persons around the world is equivalent in size to the conviction rates of rare crimes, such as homicides in Iceland (0.3 convicted per 100,000 persons) or kidnapping in Norway (0.14).

A regional overview of conviction rates seems to confirm the trend identified in terms of number of convictions, which showed that Europe had better results as far as convictions for trafficking in persons are concerned.

The figures are generally extremely low and serious debate is needed as to the reasons why the conviction rates for trafficking in persons remain at the same levels as rare crimes.

Summing up, questions may be raised as to the reasons

FIG. 55: **Conviction rate distribution among the countries reporting some convictions, 2010**

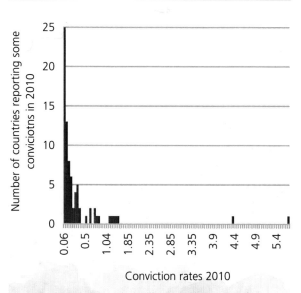

Source: UNODC elaboration on national data.

FIG. 56: **Conviction rates for trafficking in persons 2010; average by region**

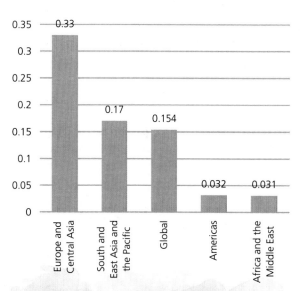

Source: UNODC elaboration on national data.

for such low conviction rates: is it because trafficking in persons is not addressed properly by the criminal justice systems or is it because it is not a widespread form of crime?

A response can be provided with a certain level of approximation by comparing the number of convictions recorded for trafficking in persons and the estimated number of victims of trafficking in persons. The 2005 and 2012 esti-

mates of the International Labour Organization (ILO) on victims of forced labour, which also includes trafficking victims, indicate that millions of victims are exploited as a result of trafficking. In light of these estimates, it appears that the criminal justice response is extremely weak compared to the scale of the problem.

In 2009, the Executive Director of UNODC noted in his foreword to that year's *Global Report on Trafficking in Per-*

The UNODC Human Trafficking Case law database

The UNODC Human Trafficking Case law database aims at assisting judges and prosecutors by making available details of real cases with examples of how the respective national laws can be used to prosecute trafficking in persons. The case law database aims to address the lack of knowledge and understanding of how to make use of the definition of trafficking in persons. Very little is currently known internationally about the cases where prosecutions have been carried out. How do practitioners use the respective laws and what - if any - are the characteristics of successful prosecutions? In a bid to answer these questions, UNODC has developed a human trafficking case law database to provide immediate, public access to officially documented instances of this crime. The database contains details on victims' and perpetrators' nationalities, trafficking routes, verdicts and other information related to prosecuted cases from across the world. It provides not only mere statistics on the numbers of prosecutions and convictions, but also the real-life stories of trafficked persons as documented by the courts. At its launch, more than 200 selected cases from over 40 countries and two regional courts were uploaded, with more added in subsequent months. Such a database of human trafficking cases enables users to take experiences and court decisions from other countries into account when dealing with human trafficking issues, consult on practices in different jurisdictions and broaden their knowledge of human trafficking crimes.

sons that, "the number of convictions is increasing, but not proportionately to the growing awareness (and probably, size) of the problem. (…) as of 2007/08, two out of every five countries covered by this report had not recorded a single conviction. Either they are blind to the problem, or they are ill-equipped to deal with it."

In the Global Plan of Action, Member States resolved to take concrete actions to strengthen their capacity *inter alia* to identify victims of trafficking in persons, enhance efforts to investigate alleged cases, strengthen means to combat trafficking, prosecute perpetrators, and to investigate, prosecute and punish corrupt officials who engage in or facilitate trafficking in persons.

Beyond adopting legislation in line with the Trafficking in Persons Protocol, Member States need to increase the capacity of their criminal justice systems to implement the Protocol and, in particular, to make use of its definition in practice. Many anti-trafficking actors have raised the issue of the difficulties encountered in actually using the definition of trafficking in persons. The difficulties are generated by some misunderstandings about what the definition is and what its constituent elements are, what the criminal act of trafficking in persons is, as well as by problems in defining some of its key concepts.

In order to make use of existing legislation, law enforcement personnel, border control officers, labour inspectors, consular and embassy officials, judges and prosecutors and peacekeepers all need to be aware of the crime of trafficking in persons and have the technical knowledge to refer incidents to appropriate authorities or to undertake investigations. Implementing legislation in practice is what ensures impact.

Core results – Criminal justice responses: status of legislation and convictions

- 134 countries and territories in the world have criminalized trafficking with a specific offence in line with the Trafficking in Persons Protocol.

- In 2012, the percentage of countries without an offence criminalizing trafficking in persons has more than halved compared to 2008.

- Among countries with no legislation or legislation with partial criminalization - 28 countries in total - African States accounted for 60 per cent.

- The number of countries in Africa and the Middle East to include a specific and comprehensive offence on trafficking in persons in domestic legislation increased from 16 in 2008 to 33 in 2012.

- The number of convictions is very low: among 132 countries, 16 per cent did not record a single conviction between 2007 and 2010.

- However, more countries reported increases than decreases in the number of convictions between 2007 and 2010.

- Africa and the Middle East is the region where less convictions were recorded. About 40 per cent of countries in this region did not record a single conviction during the reporting period.

- In Asia and Europe the percentage of countries where no convictions are recorded has been reduced to about 5 per cent and 2 per cent, respectively.

- The conviction rates for trafficking in persons remain at the same levels of rare crimes such as homicides in Iceland or kidnapping in Norway.

B. CHALLENGES TO THE IMPLEMENTATION OF COMPREHENSIVE RESPONSES TO TRAFFICKING IN PERSONS

While the growing number of States Parties to the Trafficking in Persons Protocol is a reflection of the political will of Member States to combat human trafficking, ratification in itself is not sufficient to ensure its effective implementation and impact on the ground, as shown above with the status of the criminal justice responses.

The first and foremost challenge identified at all levels in the practical implementation of anti-human trafficking activities is the allocation of sufficient financial resources. Beyond this cross-cutting and over-arching challenge which all stakeholders face particularly in times of financial and economical crises, the main topical challenges identified in prevention, protection and prosecution efforts lie in the following three areas: (a) knowledge and research, (b) capacity building and development and (c) monitoring and evaluation. The following section summarizes some of the main internationally recognized challenges faced in the implementation of comprehensive responses to trafficking in persons.[47] It lays foundations for analysing the Global Plan of Action in light of address-

47 This section relies on the following publications: UNODC, *International Framework for Action to Implement the Trafficking in Persons Protocol*, 2009 and OHCHR, UNHCR, UNICEF, UNODC, UN Women and ILO, *Prevent, Combat, Protect – Human Trafficking. A Joint UN Commentary on the EU Directive – A Human Rights-Based Approach* (2011), pp. 24-29.

ing challenges that have remained since the adoption of the Trafficking in Persons Protocol.

1. Lack of knowledge and research

One of the most persistent issues on the human trafficking agenda has been the lack of knowledge about the phenomenon. The Report of the Special Body of Experts on Traffic in Women and Children, which was established under the League of Nations, stated the following in 1927:[48]

> "Those whose duty it has been to grapple with the traffic in women, whether as Government officials or as members of voluntary associations, are faced with doubts of a different character. Their experiences forces them to believe that the evil which for so many years has resisted the constant attempts of many countries to uproot it must still exist; but the extent of its operations and precise form which it assumes at the present time are to them matters of uncertainty."

After 1927 and particularly after the adoption of the Trafficking in Persons Protocol in 2000, the number of studies on human trafficking has boomed. Unfortunately, because of the uneven quality of these studies they have not always contributed to increase the knowledge on trafficking. Based on a comprehensive literature review carried out in 2008, out of 2,388 publications, only 741 met a basic level of scientific rigour and most of them did not use a solid methodology.[49] In spite of the problems with the quality of human trafficking research, there is also much reliable data on human trafficking which has been collected by using quantitative or qualitative methods.[50]

Member States and other actors dealing with trafficking in persons have emphasized time and again that in order to be efficient, the responses to trafficking should be evidence based. Research has the role of providing this evidence and increasing the knowledge on needs, successful actions and impact of interventions. Reliable knowledge of and research into the specific national, regional and international trafficking in persons context is a prerequisite for the elaboration, implementation and evaluation of anti-human trafficking strategies and development of evidence-based policies. Knowledge and research are also

paramount to overcoming the current partial understanding of the crime and the violations of human rights it entails.

In order to strengthen national, regional and global efforts to fight human trafficking, a better understanding of the scope and nature of this crime is needed. Although most countries have adopted a specific criminal offence on trafficking in persons, there is still a diversity of interpretations of and approaches to the Trafficking in Persons Protocol and the definition used by Member States. Some only acknowledge certain forms of exploitation or certain categories of victims or criminals. The result of the varied ways of interpreting the Protocol is that countries may not refer to same practices when referring to human trafficking cases, thereby limiting the scope and effectiveness of the response and hindering international cooperation. This also has an impact on data collection since countries may report the same trafficking patterns in a different way, making it difficult to form a clear picture of efficient practices.

Actors in the fight against trafficking in persons agree that some key concepts of the trafficking in persons definition need further analysis and research in order to allow for better implementation.[51] One of these elements is vulnerability. In the context of the definition of trafficking in persons, criminal justice practitioners in particular find it difficult to tackle the elements of "abuse of a position of vulnerability" and "abuse of power" which are prescribed means by which trafficking in persons can take place. In order to successfully assist vulnerable populations to protect themselves from potentially harmful situations, it is essential to understand what makes them vulnerable to violence, abuse and exploitation in the first place. Preventing trafficking in persons is largely based on reducing vulnerability and providing options to avoid potentially harmful situations leading to trafficking.[52] That is why the understanding of vulnerability and the abuse of power connected to vulnerability is vital for the development of successful strategies against trafficking in persons.[53]

••

48 League of Nations 1927, p9.

49 Gozdziak, E. M., and Bump, M. N., *Data and Research on Human Trafficking: Bibliography of Research-Based Literature*, Georgetown University, Washington D.C., 2008.

50 See, for example, UN.GIFT.HUB, Publications (http://www.ungift.org/knowledgehub/publications.html)

51 UNODC, *International Framework for Action for the Implementation of the Trafficking in Persons Protocol*, 2009, p. 5.

52 Clark, M.A., 'Vulnerability, Prevention and Human Trafficking – The Need for a new Paradigm,' in UNODC, *An Introduction to Human Trafficking: Vulnerability, Impact and Action*, (2008).

53 Recommendations from the Working Group on Trafficking in Persons, established by the Conference of the Parties to the Convention against Transnational Organized Crime, concerning vulnerability was presented in October 2012 (CTOC/COP/WG 4/2011/3 Analysis of key concepts: focus on the concept of 'abuse of power or of a position of vulnerability' in Article 3, Trafficking in Persons Protocol).

Lack of knowledge hinders effective implementation of anti-trafficking policies and strategies, since often they are based on political, social and economic agendas rather than actual facts. However, it should be kept in mind that data collection on trafficking in persons is a challenging task which requires focused and continuous efforts to keep the knowledge base updated. The harmonization of the fight against trafficking in persons starts from a common understanding of what is dealt with, and through the ability to compare situations by using evidence and research.

2. Lack of capacity

Member States are faced with different challenges in preventing and combating trafficking in persons, not only because the extent and nature of the problem varies but also due to different capacities across countries and regions. As shown above, some countries, particularly in Africa and the Middle East, face difficulties in criminal justice responses including sufficient legislation and number of convictions. Strengthening capacity at the national level is necessary for countries to obtain the institutional and technical ability to develop, implement and assess their own anti-human trafficking policies and strategies. In view of the complex and changing nature of the crime, it is also essential that countries are able to strengthen, adapt and maintain the required capacity over time.

In order to combat trafficking in persons and its transnational or national organized crime component, coordination and cooperation is a basic requirement. Therefore, in addition to training and capacity building at the national level, exchanges of good practices and cooperation and coordination with partners in other countries has been recognized as crucial to ensure a sustained and long-term response to trafficking in persons. This, in turn, helps ensure that isolated responses to the crime do not simply result in the problem being diverted elsewhere.

Combating trafficking in persons requires capacity to implement a comprehensive approach. Such an approach requires the contribution of trained staff from a very wide range of authorities and sectors. A lot of people may potentially represent the 'last chance' for a victim of trafficking in persons of being detected. As many people as possible must have the capacity to identify victims, know

how to deal with them, and how to refer them to the relevant protection and assistance services. These professionals may also significantly support the investigation and prosecution of traffickers, directly or indirectly.

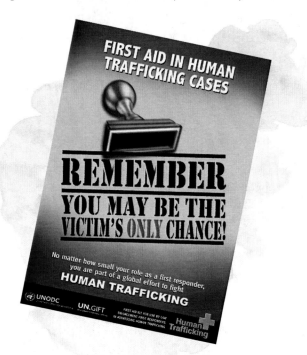

The importance of capacity building is widely recognized and in many countries significant efforts to train professionals are currently in place. However, in many sectors and institutions, the flow of resources to other sectors through a high turnover of civil servants has consequences for the sustainability of resources which makes capacity building particularly difficult. Also, in many parts of the world countries are struggling with a plethora of problems, and trafficking in persons is simply only one of the many concerns requiring resources and capacities.

3. Lack of monitoring and evaluation

As there has been a boom of studies on human trafficking there has also been an increasing number of initiatives to respond to trafficking in persons. Unfortunately, there is still relatively little knowledge of the effectiveness of these efforts since their impact has seldom been evaluated. In order to establish a baseline to evaluate any progress in the implementation of policies, strategies and programmes, systematically collected knowledge on national, regional and global patterns and trends is needed, and this also helps to monitor the changes in human trafficking

••

Based on the recommendations of the Working Group and the call for further analysis of the key concepts of the Trafficking in Persons Protocol contained in Resolution 5/2 of the Conference of the States Parties UNODC has published an Issue Paper on *Abuse of position of vulnerability and other "means" within the definition of trafficking in persons*, 2012.

situations. This is crucial for different stakeholders to provide an appropriate response to trafficking in persons.

Despite the relatively modest efforts to evaluate the activities connected to trafficking in persons, the need to assess the impact of activities and projects implemented is generally recognized. Are preventive efforts helping to decrease the number of victims of trafficking in persons? Is the provision of training sustainable and is it increasing the capacity for action? Are the protective initiatives ensuring safety and strengthening the rights of victims? How can it be ensured that awareness-raising campaigns are appropriately targeted to have a positive impact? Countries must be able to offer answers to questions such as these in appropriately targeting responses. Not only do Member States need to know whether their anti-trafficking policies and activities are effective, but so too does the United Nations system as well as other international, regional and non-governmental organizations, and actors such as the private sector.

Stakeholders have great difficulties measuring the impact of anti-trafficking in persons activities. The cost implications of building in a baseline component in some activities are very high, particularly in light of the fact that trafficking situations change quickly and resources are scarce.

Also, one should not forget that monitoring and evaluation of anti-trafficking activities are often not institutionalized functions of national authorities but linked to specific projects implemented by external partners. Once these projects are finished, despite the emphasis on generating sustainable outcomes, the monitoring and evaluation of these outcomes post-project often disappear.

C. ADDRESSING THE CHALLENGES – THE GLOBAL PLAN OF ACTION

Faced with recurring challenges, Member States decided to ensure that the next steps in the fight against trafficking in persons were taken without denying the positive impact of the Trafficking in Persons Protocol. In 2010, just a few months short of the tenth anniversary of the adoption of the Protocol, Member States renewed their commitment to the fight against trafficking in persons when the General Assembly adopted the *United Nations Global Plan of Action to Combat Trafficking in Persons* (A/RES/64/293).

When negotiating the Global Plan of Action, Member States were armed with overarching principles drawn from international standards and norms or recognized as good practices, which provided the backdrop to their action. Only an approach that entails respect for human rights and non-discrimination was seen as having the potential to succeed, which means that any strategy to combat trafficking in persons should be gender and child sensitive, and should aim at being sustainable, evidence-based and interdisciplinary. In order for initiatives to be in line with efforts by other countries, they should be anchored in the Trafficking in Persons Protocol. With the Global Plan of Action, Member States committed to a multidisciplinary and integrated approach to ending trafficking in persons so that it is placed in the broader context of development, peace, security and human rights.[54]

Following the principles of the Trafficking in Persons Protocol, Member States' renewed commitment through the Global Plan of Action includes action using the commonly known approach of the "4 Ps": preventing trafficking in persons; protecting and assisting the victims; prosecuting the traffickers; and building partnerships. With a view to supporting implementation of the Trafficking in Persons Protocol, the Global Plan of Action was focused on helping Member States reinforce their political commitments and legal obligations to prevent and combat trafficking in persons and encourage them to promote comprehensive, coordinated and consistent responses, at the national, regional and international levels. Member States also laid the ground to promoting a human rights-based, gender- and age-sensitive approach in addressing factors that make people vulnerable to trafficking in persons and strengthening the criminal justice response.

Support of UNODC to bridge the implementation gap

UNODC started its anti-trafficking work in 1999 with the Global Programme against Trafficking in Persons. Since then, UNODC has supported Member States in their fight against human trafficking in cooperation with other international and regional organizations in the fields of research and awareness raising, capacity building and the promotion of partnerships and inter-agency coordination. Following are some examples of initiatives that aim at supporting the Member States to implement the Trafficking in Persons Protocol and the Global Plan of Action.

54   Introduction to the Annex, United Nations Global Plan of Action to Combat Trafficking in Persons.

The United Nations Global Plan of Action to Combat Trafficking in Persons

The Global Plan of Action requests that Member States and the international community take action against trafficking in persons in the following areas:

Prevention of trafficking in persons

Address factors that make people vulnerable:
* Poverty
* Unemployment
* Inequality
* Humanitarian emergencies (armed conflicts, natural disasters)
* Sexual violence
* Gender discrimination
* Social exclusion
* Marginalisation
* Culture of tolerance against violence against women, youth and children

Address all forms of trafficking in persons.

Include trafficking in persons in the United Nations work on:
* Economic and social development
* Human rights
* Rule of law
* Good governance
* Education and natural disaster
* Post-conflict reconstruction

Implement comprehensive policies and action in line with policies on:
* Migration
* Education
* Employment
* Gender equality
* Empowerment of women
* Crime prevention

Conduct research and share best practices.

Develop process for the identification of victims and reinforce the provision of identity documents.

Promote awareness raising to discourage the demand and promote human rights education.

Focus on demand and trafficking for labour exploitation, and educate consumers on goods and services produced as a result of trafficking in persons.

Strengthen the capacity of law enforcement, immigration, education, social welfare, labour and other relevant officials to prevent trafficking in persons, in cooperation with civil society.

Protection of and assistance to victims of trafficking in persons

Promote and protect the rights of victims, reintegrate them into the community and treat them as victims of crime making sure that they are not penalized for having been trafficked.

Review and strengthen services and referral mechanisms.

Strengthen the capacity of those likely to encounter victims:
Law enforcement personnel; border control officers; labour inspectors; consular or embassy officials; judges and prosecutors; peacekeepers and other relevant sectors including civil society.

Protect the privacy and identity of victims and ensure their safety as well the safety of their family members.

Provide assistance and services for the physical, psychological and social recovery and rehabilitation of trafficked persons including special services such as access to prevention, treatment, care and support services for HIV and AIDS and other blood-borne and communicable diseases.

Consider adopting measures to permit victims to remain in destination countries.

Ensure a safe and preferably voluntary return of victims to their origin country.

Adopt labour laws which provide legal rights and protections for workers that would limit their risk of being trafficked.

Provide appropriate assistance and protection in the best interest of the child to child victims.

Establish the United Nations Voluntary Trust Fund for Victims of Trafficking in Persons.

Adopt measures for compensation.

Acknowledge the important role of civil society organizations.

Ensure victims' access to justice.

Provide victims with a reflection period.

Prosecution of crimes of trafficking in persons

Criminalize and prosecute all forms of trafficking in persons including attempting, participating and directing other persons to commit an offence as well as organized criminal groups' involvement in trafficking in persons.

Ensure the liability of all categories of perpetrators of trafficking in persons, including the liability of legal persons and entities.

Enhance investigation and prosecution and ensure proportionate penalties: use systematically freezing and confiscation of assets .

Make use of the available technical assistance.

Investigate, prosecute and punish corrupt public officials who engage in trafficking in persons and promote a zero-tolerance policy against corruption.

Strengthen cooperation among countries to address crimes that can be linekd to trafficking in persons

such as money-laundering, corruption, smuggling of migrants and all forms of organized crime.

Exchange information among relevant authorities.

Strengthening of partnerships against trafficking in persons

Enhance cooperation among UN bodies and other international organizations particularly in relation to capacity building.

Support the Inter-Agency Coordination Group against Trafficking in Persons; Encourage UN bodies and other international organizations to assist Member States and improve the coherence and efficiency of delivery.

Encourage cooperation, share of best practices and mutual legal assistance at the national, bilateral, regional and international levels.

Promote cooperation among different stakeholders such as authorities, civil society, private sector, media, workers' and employers' organizations and law enforcement agencies.

Requests UNODC to collect information and report biannually on patterns and flows of trafficking in persons.

Secure funding for the work of the UN against human trafficking.

The Blue Heart Campaign raises awareness of trafficking in persons and inspire those with decision-making power to effect change. Through the campaign, a number of Member States have promoted awareness raising for the general public.

On the research side, the first *Global Report on Trafficking in Persons* was published in 2009.[55] The present report is the first in a series of biannual reports on human trafficking patterns and trends following the mandate of the Global Plan of Action. Also, a series of issue papers has

been launched to addresses such specific themes as the vulnerability; the role of corruption in trafficking in persons; organized crime involvement in trafficking in persons and smuggling of migrants; and combating trafficking in persons in accordance with the principles of Islamic law.[56]

Through its technical cooperation work, UNODC has been supporting Member States by providing legislative assistance, advice on strategic planning and policy development, strengthening criminal justice responses and improving protection and support to victims of trafficking in persons. The work has particularly aimed at strengthening the capacities of Member States and to that end, UNODC has created an anti-trafficking in persons global training initiative to improve the delivery of relevant trainings.

55   UNODC/UN.GIFT (2009).

56   See http://www.unodc.org/unodc/en/human-trafficking/publications.html?ref=menuside#Issue_Papers.

Compensation for victims of trafficking in persons

The third session of the Working Group on Trafficking in Persons of the Conference of the Parties to the United Nations Convention against Transnational Organized Crime addressed the issue of compensation mentioned also in the Global Plan of Action: "adopt measures to ensure that victims of trafficking in persons can seek compensation for the damage suffered, consistent with the Convention and the Trafficking in Persons Protocol". The Working Group made a series of recommendations developing the type of measures which can be adopted to ensure access to compensation. These measures include the facilitation of the provision of legal assistance and information regarding legal assistance to victims of trafficking in order to represent their interests in criminal investigations, including in order to obtain compensation. Legal assistance should also endeavor to integrate at the beginning of the penal investigation a section dedicated to the property and assets of traffickers and the possibility of seizing and confiscating good obtained by criminal means.

The Group also recommended that the availability of compensation be ensured independent of a criminal case and regardless of whether the offender can be identified, sentenced and punished. The Group further detailed the types of costs that should be considered to be covered by court ordered and/or state-funded compensation:

  (i) Costs of medical, physical, psychological or psychiatric treatment required by the victim;

 (ii) Costs of physical and occupational therapy or rehabilitation required by the victim;

(iii) Lost income and wages due according to national law and regulations regarding wages;

(iv) Legal fees and other costs or expenses incurred, including costs related to the participation of the victim in the criminal investigation and prosecution process;

 (v) Payment for non-material damages resulting from moral, physical or psychological injury, emotional distress and pain and suffering of the victim as a result of the crime committed against him or her;

(vi) Any other costs or losses incurred by the victim as a direct result of being trafficked, as reasonably assessed by the court or state-funded compensation scheme.

Non-governmental organizations and other elements of civil society are well acknowledged partners in the fight against trafficking in persons. The Voluntary Trust Fund, established in 2010, dedicates funds to NGOs in recognition of their crucial role as providers of direct assistance to victims of trafficking in persons. The first Small Grants Facility of the Trust Fund supported 12 projects led by an NGO or a consortium of NGOs in Albania, Cambodia, Costa Rica, Czech Republic, France, Israel, Kenya, Nepal, Nigeria, Republic of Moldova and the United States of America.

Joint efforts of the United Nations system are coordinated and strengthened within the Inter-agency Coordination Group against Trafficking in Persons (ICAT) and the

UNITED NATIONS
VOLUNTARY TRUST FUND
FOR VICTIMS OF
HUMAN TRAFFICKING

United Nations Global Initiative to Fight Human Trafficking (UN.GIFT), as well as at the regional and subregional levels and within the Global Migration Group. All these efforts ensure that coordination and cooperation is addressed and that trafficking in persons is taken into consideration in fora where it may not have the primary focus.

D. MEASURING THE IMPACT OF ANTI-TRAFFICKING EFFORTS

So much has been achieved, yet as some of the outcomes of this report show, much remains to be done by the international community to fully implement a comprehensive approach to trafficking in persons following the four Ps recalled in the Global Plan of Action: Prevention, Protection and assistance, Prosecution and Partnerships.

Since the negotiations of the Transnational Organized Crime Convention and its Protocols, the international community has made considerable efforts towards combating trafficking in persons. Many international organizations have a mandate which relates to trafficking in persons. A study in 2004 carried out in the context of the United Nations System Chief Executives Board (CEB)[57], showed that 17 international organizations had a mandate more or less closely related to trafficking in persons.[58] International organizations are not the only actors in the fight against trafficking in persons; Member States are at the centre of it. Many regional organizations have plans of action to combat trafficking in persons or address it in the framework of the fight against serious crime. Countless non-governmental organizations provide assistance and protection to victims of trafficking in persons, supporting their recovery, rehabilitation and reintegration in society. In addition media, businesses and individuals play a crucial role.

Many were already addressing trafficking in persons prior to 2000. But the Trafficking in Persons Protocol enabled all actors to have a common basis to combat trafficking in persons and thus be more efficient. So many projects have been undertaken, and many publications, tools and various training materials are available. Member States

have developed strategies and programmes to implement activities.

However, today, 12 years after the adoption of the Trafficking in Persons Protocol, though it is safe to say that most of the tools to combat trafficking in persons are available, how much is known about the real impact of our efforts? Is there enough information to know which practices are good in the long run and whether those identified at one point are still valid a few years later? Is there enough knowledge about what has been undertaken worldwide by all stakeholders to know that some good practices are not left aside?

Over the past decade, several Member States, international organizations and other relevant stakeholders have wondered about the impact of the strategies, policies and activities implemented. As noted by the International Organization for Migration in 2008 in its *Handbook on performance indicators for counter trafficking projects*:

"To date, the global monitoring and evaluation of counter-trafficking projects has generally been non-standardized and output (not impact) focused."

Nowadays, most programmes and projects are to be managed on the basis of results, and most strive to utilize specific indicators for each objective linked to a specific timeframe, baseline and target values. Governments, the donor community and the general public increasingly request for international organizations and other actors to account for their achievements in terms of concrete results. Yet it remains difficult when the baseline does not exist and the research necessary to acquire it would double or triple the budget of the activity for which a limited amount of funds is available.

However such indicators in the context of trafficking in persons projects and programmes and in general play an important role in measuring the impact of activities carried out and supporting the accountability of the organization. Such indicators should be specific, measurable, achievable, relevant and time-bound in order to offer a basis for evaluating anti-trafficking projects. Another approach is based on the premise that impact assessments should not refer to the immediate outputs of a project or programme but to any lasting or significant changes that it brought about.[59]

57 CEB is the prime instrument for supporting and reinforcing the coordinating role of United Nations intergovernmental bodies on social, economic and related matters.

58 Office of the High Commissioner for Human Rights (OHCHR), Division for the Advancement of Women (DAW) and United Nations Development Fund for Women (UNIFEM) – both now part of UN Women, Department of Peacekeeping Operations (DPKO), United Nations Interregional Crime and Justice Research Institute (UNICRI), Office of the United Nations High Commissioner for Refugees (UNHCR), United Nations Population Fund (UNFPA), Joint United Nations Programme on HIV/AIDS (UNAIDS), United Nations Development Programme (UNDP), United Nations Children's Fund (UNICEF), United Nations Office on Drugs and Crime (UNODC), International Organization for Migration (IOM), World Health Organization (WHO), International Labour Organization (ILO), United Nations Educational, Scientific and Cultural Organization (UNESCO), International Civil Aviation Organization (ICAO) and ICPO-Interpol.

59 Roche, C.J.R., *Impact Assessment for Development Agencies: Learning the value of change*, Oxfam, 2000.

Member States have also identified the need to monitor their anti trafficking in persons activities. Most Countries do so through the development of national plans of action. Through the data collection exercise, UNODC received national plans of action from over 40 countries. Most of the national plans of action follow the 4 Ps – Prosecution, Protection, Prevention and almost always include provisions for the enhancement of Partnerships at the national, regional and international levels. While a few countries are already implementing their second or third plan of action, it is not clear how the implementation of the first or second one was evaluated.

Most of the national plans of action have a timeline, ranging from two to five years. Some do not indicate a timeframe. Very few national plans of action include provisions on monitoring and evaluation and even less indicate the cost implications of the activities and the source of funds. Some national plans of action include research and data collection activities but not enough to indicate that research and data collection is given particular attention by Member States. Often the timeline for implementation of activities foreseen under the national plan of action is missing and so are the means of verification. From the sample of national plans of action received, it is difficult to see that specific, measurable, achievable, relevant and time-bound indicators are used.

Recognizing the difficulties in measuring the impact of anti-trafficking in persons activities by stakeholders and also the costs implications of building in a baseline component in some activities (particularly in light of the fact that trafficking situations change quickly and resources are scarce), it is key to ensure that all stakeholders cooperate to support better reporting and impact assessment. The development of national plans of action by Member States is an indication that there is a wish to establish work plans in order to check that the activities carried out are contributing to a comprehensive response to trafficking in persons. Regional mechanisms are also engaging in the development of regional plans of action, some complemented by national plans of action.

The International Framework for Action to Implement the Trafficking in Persons Protocol[60] provides a basis for Member States to review their policy and assess the progress made in the implementation of a comprehensive response to trafficking in persons taking into considera-

tion the requirements of the Protocol as well as other relevant international instruments.

Aware of the need to be able to review the progress made and results achieved, Member States have been discussing a review mechanism for the United Nations Convention against Transnational Organized Crime and its three additional Protocols. Some of the guiding principles and characteristics of the mechanism are: to provide opportunities to share good practices and challenges; to assist States in the effective implementation of the Convention and the Protocols; and to identify difficulties encountered by States parties in the fulfilment of their obligations.

The movement towards reflecting on what has been done and ensuring that activities carried out take into consideration lessons learned and reviewing the impact of anti-trafficking in persons activities is growing. The objective is not to rank countries, organizations or any other stakeholders, but rather to ensure that funds are well-spent and that activities have a positive impact on the ground. Similar to Member States, the international community is determined to prevent and combat trafficking in persons, protect and assist victims, prosecute crimes of trafficking in persons and promote partnerships through concrete actions. At the level of the United Nations system, the establishment of the Special Rapporteur on Trafficking in Persons, showed the commitment to monitoring the work of Member States.

The implementation of the Global Plan of Action is to be appraised in 2013. In light of the present report and the activities undertaken by Member States, the United Nations system and other relevant international organizations, the General Assembly will address the next steps.

These concrete actions are aimed at having an identifiable and positive impact on the trafficking in persons situation worldwide. A harmonized understanding of trafficking in persons and all its facets is at the basis of all coordination and cooperation. The entry into force of the Trafficking in Persons Protocol has shown an impact on the legislative framework of Member States, as well as to some extent on the criminal justice system. Member States have renewed their commitment by adopting the Global Plan of Action.

Our work is not yet done. For the sake of victims of trafficking in persons and of States plagued by transnational organized crime, all actors have to continue working together to achieve the goal set out by the General Assembly: end the heinous crime of trafficking in persons.

---

60 Available at http://www.unodc.org/documents/human-trafficking/Framework_for_Action_TIP.pdf.

REFERENCES

Bundeslagebild Menschenhandel (2000-2010) Bundeskriminalamt. Available at: http://www.bka.de/DE/ThemenABisZ/Deliktsbereiche/Menschenhandel/Lagebilder/lagebilder__node.html?__nnn=true

Carchedi, F. and Orfano, I. (2007) La tratta di persone in Italia: Evoluzione del fenomeno ed ambiti di sfruttamento, Milan, FrancoAngeli.

Carling, J. (2005) Migration, Human Smuggling and Trafficking from Nigeria to Europe, Geneva, IOM.

Ciconte, E. (2005). The trafficking flows and routes of Eastern Europe, WEST Project ref. N. 2A071. Bologna, WEST.

Clark, M.A. (2008) Vulnerability, Prevention and Human Trafficking: The Need for a new Paradigm. In United Nations Office on Drugs and Crime, An Introduction to Human Trafficking: Vulnerability, Impact and Action, Vienna, UNODC.

Conference of the Parties to the Convention against Transnational Organized Crime (2011) Working Group on Trafficking in Persons, CTOC/COP/WG.4/2011/3, Analysis of key concepts: focus on the concept of "abuse of power or of a position of vulnerability" in article 3 of the Protocol to Prevent, Suppress and Punish Trafficking in Persons, Especially Women and Children, supplementing the United Nations Convention against Transnational Organized Crime, Background paper prepared by the Secretariat.

Convention to Suppress the Slave Trade and Slavery, September 25, 1926. League of Nations Treaty Series, March 9, 1927.

Denisova, T. (2004) Trafficking in Women and Children for Purposes of Sexual Exploitation, Zaporizhie State University. Available at: http://www.childtrafficking.com/Docs/denisova__no_date___traffic.pdf

Department of Families, Housing, Community Services and Indigenous Affairs, Australian Government. Available at: http://www.fahcsia.gov.au/

Directorate of Women and Children Service Centre, Nepal Police. Available at: http://www.nepalpolice.gov.np/

Dutch National Rapporteur (2000-2010) Trafficking in Human Beings, First, Second, Third, and Fourth reports. Den Haag, Bureau NRM.

Economic and Social Council resolution 1984/48, Crime prevention and criminal justice in the context of development", 25 May 1984.

Egyptian National Center for Social and Criminological Research (2010) Trafficking in Human Beings in the Egyptian Society: Patterns, Variables and Actors. Available at: www.ncscr.org.eg

Fiscalia General de la Republica de El Salvador. Available at: http://www.fgr.gob.sv/

Forced Labour Convention, 1930 (No. 29), of the International Labour Organization (United Nations, Treaty Series, vol. 39, No. 612).

General Assembly resolution 64/293, United Nations Global Plan of Action to Combat Trafficking in Persons, 12 August 2010.

General Assembly resolution 55/25, United Nations Convention against Transnational Organized Crime,15 November 2000.

Gozdziak, E. M., & Bump, M. N. (2008) Data and Research on Human Trafficking: Bibliography of Research-Based Literature, Institute for the Study of International Migration, Walsh School of Foreign Service, Georgetown University.

Hughes, D.M. and Denisova, T. (2002) Trafficking in Women from Ukraine. Available at: https://www.ncjrs.gov/pdffiles1/nij/grants/203275.pdf

Inter-Agency Coordination Group against Trafficking in Persons (2010) An analytical review - 10 years on from the adoption of the United Nations Trafficking in Persons Protocol. Available at: http://www.unodc.org/documents/human-trafficking/ICAT_Backgound_Paper.pdf

International Organization for Migration (2008) No Experience Necessary: The Internal Trafficking of Persons in South Africa, Pretoria, IOM.

International Organization for Migration (2001) Deceived Migrants from Tajikistan: A Study of Trafficking in Women and Children, Dushanbe, IOM.

Legal and Human Rights Centre (2010) Tanzania Human Rights Report 2009, LHRC.

Ministry of Health, Labour and Welfare, Government of Japan. Available at: http://www.mhlw.go.jp/english/

Ministry of Justice, Government of Denmark. Available at: http://www.justitsministeriet.dk/generelt/english

Ministry of Justice, Government of Japan. Available at: http://www.moj.go.jp/ENGLISH/

National Agency for the Prohibition of Traffic in Persons (NAPTIP), Federal Government of Nigeria. Available at: http://www.naptip.gov.ng/index.html

National Committee for Combating Human Trafficking, Sultanate of Oman. Available at: http://www.ncchtoman.gov.om/english/default.asp

National Police Agency (NPA), Government of Japan. Available at: http://www.npa.go.jp/english/index.htm

National Prosecuting Authority of South Africa (2010) Tsireledzani: Understanding the dimensions of human trafficking in Southern Africa, Research report, NPA. Available at: http://www.hsrc.ac.za/Document-3562.phtml

Organization for Security and Cooperation in Europe and the United Nations Global Initiative to Fight Human Trafficking (2010) Analysing the Business Model of Trafficking in Human Beings to Better Prevent the Crime, Vienna, OSCE.

Prevent, Combat, Protect – Human Trafficking (2011) A Joint UN Commentary on the EU Directive – A Human Rights-Based Approach, OHCHR, UNHCR, UNICEF, UNODC, UN Women and ILO.

Roche, C.J.R. (2000) Impact Assessment for Development Agencies : Learning the value of change, Oxfam.

Royal Canadian Mounted Police, Human Trafficking in Canada: A Threat Assessment, 2010. Available at: http://www.rcmp-grc.gc.ca/pubs/ht-tp/htta-tpem-eng.htm.

Siegel, D. and de Blank, S. (2010) 'Women who traffic women: the role of women in human trafficking networks – Dutch cases, Global Crime, 11:4, November 2010.

Siliadin v France (2005) EHRLR 660 (para 123), the European Court of Human Rights.

Surtees, R. (2008) Traffickers and Trafficking in Southern and Eastern Europe, European Journal of Criminology, Volume5 (1).

Travaux Préparatoires of the Negotiations for the Elaboration of the United Nations Convention against Transnational Organized Crime and the Protocols Thereto (2006) Vienna, UNODC.

UN Women (2011) Progress of the World's Women 2011-2012: in Pursuit of Justice, New York. Available at: http://progress.unwomen.org/pdfs/EN-Report-Progress.pdf

UN.GIFT.HUB, Publications. Available at: http://www.ungift.org/knowledgehub/publications.html

UNICRI (2005) Trafficking in Women from Romania into Germany: Comprehensive Report, United Nations Interregional Crime and Justice Research Institute Turin, UNICRI.

UNICRI (2004) Trafficking of Nigerian Girls to Italy = Traffico delle ragazze nigeriane in Italia, United Nations Interregional Crime and Justice Research Institute, Turin, UNICRI.

United Nations Convention against Transnational Organized Crime, United Nations, Treaty Series, vol. 2237, No. 39574. Available at: http://www.unodc.org/unodc/en/treaties/CTOC/index.html#Fulltext

United Nations Development Programme/Ministry of Home Affairs(2011) Public Safety and Parliamentary Affairs, Rapid Assessment of Trafficking in Persons in Lesotho.

United Nations Office on Drugs and Crime (2012) Abuse of a position of vulnerability and other "means" within the definition of trafficking in persons, Issue Paper, Vienna, UNODC.

United Nations Office on Drugs and Crime (2009) International Framework for Action for the Implementation of the Trafficking in Persons Protocol, Vienna, UNODC. Available at: http://www.unodc.org/documents/human-trafficking/Framework_for_Action_TIP.pdf

United Nations Office on Drugs and Crime (2007) An Assessment of Referral Practices to Assist and Protect the Rights of Trafficked Persons in Moldova, Chisinau, UNODC.

UNODC/UN.GIFT (2009) Global Report on Trafficking in Persons. Available at: http://www.unodc.org/unodc/en/data-and-analysis/glotip.html

World Bank, World Databank. Available at: http://databank.worldbank.org/ddp/home.do

World Health Assembly resolution WHA57.18. Human organ and tissue transplantation. Available at: http://apps.who.int/gb/ebwha/pdf_files/WHA57/A57_R18-en.pdf